MaryAnn F. Kohl
Barbara Zaborowski

Action ART

HANDS-ON ACTIVE ART
ADVENTURES

BRIGHT IDEAS
FOR LEARNING™

Bright Ring Publishing, Inc.

Credits

Bright Ring Publishing, Inc.
PO Box 31338
Bellingham, WA 98228
360-592-9201
WWW.BRIGHTRING.COM

ISBN 13 Print Book.............. 978-0935607-34-5
ISBN PDF Ebook................. 978-0935607-35-2
ISBN EPUB Ebook............... 978-0935607-37-6
ISBN Kindle Ebook.............. 978-0935607-36-9

Library of Congress Control Number: 2014915511

Publishers Cataloging in Publication Data
(Provided by Quality Books, Inc.)

Kohl, MaryAnn F.
     Action art : hands-on active art adventures / MaryAnn
F. Kohl and Barbara Zaborowski.
     pages cm – (Bright ideas for learning ; 9)
     Includes index.
     SUMMARY: Art experiences and art activities for
children and the adults who work with them.
     Audience: Ages 2-12.
     LCCN 2014915511
     ISBN 978-0935607-34-5 (print)
     ISBN 978-0935607-35-2 (PDF)
     ISBN 978-0935607-37-6 (EPUB)
     ISBN 978-0935607-36-9 (Kindle)

     1. Handicraft–Juvenile literature. 2. Creative
activities and seat work–Juvenile literature.
[1. Handicraft. 2. Creative activities and seat work.]
I. Zaborowski, Barbara, 1946- II. Title. III. Series:
Kohl, MaryAnn F. Bright ideas for learning ; 9.

TT160.K628 2015   745.5
                               QBI15-600019

Printed in China by Four Colour Print Group, Louisville, Kentucky.... June 2015

Bulk Purchases

Bright Ring Publishing books are available for special premiums and
promotions as well as for fund-raising purposes. Bulk purchases are
offered at a discount. Special editions or excerpts can be created to
specification. Contact MaryAnn F. Kohl at Bright Ring Publishing.

Disclaimer

Bright Ring Publishing, Inc. and the authors, MaryAnn F. Kohl and Barbara
Zaborowski, strongly affirm that children must be closely supervised by an
adult at all times during setup and involvement in art activities found in *Action
ART*. Proper use of and caution with art materials must be strictly followed
at all times. Children's abilities should be assessed by the adult in charge as
to each child's appropriate developmental level and ability to safely engage
in *Action ART* projects and activities. The publisher and authors assume no
responsibility or liability whatsoever for use of activities in this book, nor for
adult supervision, nor for any use of art materials by or with children.

Every effort has been made to locate permission and copyright information.

Special Thanks

Special thanks and deepest appreciation go to all the children, parents, teachers, librarians, bloggers, co-workers, family, and friends who enthusiastically joined in and made *Action ART* possible. Each of you is an important part of this book. Some will be mentioned here, and all of you will find your tributes at the end of the book, where you will be listed with your websites, blogs, art contributions, or photography contributions. Thank you, and thank you again!

- Terry Hill, for *Action ART* graphic design, Terry Hill Designs.
- Barbara Zaborowski's preschoolers, for their process artwork contributions and participation in photography.
- Naomi Yalkowsky Foster, Tucson Jewish Community Center, for the photo of her student riding a trike on the front cover.
- Vicky Perreault, owner of messforless.com, for the photograph of her Bubble Wrap boots daughter on the back cover.
- Michael Kohl, Hannah Kohl, and Megan Kohl, for cover design assistance and book direction.

Dedications

To my husband, Michael, who has always supported me with his love, time, and spectacular advice in my devotion to children's creativity.

~ MaryAnn

To my husband, Roy, who never once, in all my years of teaching preschool, suggested I get a "real" job.

~ Barbara

Introducing *Action ART*

Why *Action ART*?

Action ART brings children hands-on art experiences that involve active exploration, from tossing to snapping to jumping to running and much more. Every art experience is physically active in some way. Sometimes it's snapping a painted rubber band and sometimes it's dancing on Bubble Wrap; sometimes it's tossing cotton balls and sometimes it's popping balloons filled with paint.

The experiences are wide and varied, some using small motor skills and some using large motor skills, some noisy and some quiet, and all employing the use of the child's movements from head to toe.

We all know that children prefer to be active, and *Action ART* incorporates the child's natural need for activity with the always important need for creativity. The art experiences are based on the philosophy that children will learn from the process of creating, and that the finished product is the result of that process, not the goal. Today's educators say, "Art for children is a process, not a product." *Action ART* projects result in products to be enjoyed and admired, but it is the process of exploration and experimenting that stimulates the child's learning from discovering and creating without an adult model or sample to copy.

How is *Action ART* organized?

Action ART is organized by color-coded chapters and movement categories, such as, Chapter 1: Snapping • Squeezing • Tapping, or Chapter 3: Blowing • Exploding • Smooshing. Color-coding separates each chapter into blocks of pages. For example, Chapter 1 has green borders and headings, Chapter 2 blue, Chapter 3 aqua, and so on.

Each activity within a chapter offers helpful icons at the top of the page spread to indicate ease or challenge for the child, time required for adult prepping and planning, and symbols of what art medium is used (paint, crayon, scissors, etc.).

Each project lists materials and lists easy steps to follow. Helpful hints are found by the little orange bug who sits on the left page of each project. Photographs shows real–life action, not staged photos, that give you ideas for what may occur with your own experience.

Action ART offers a detailed resource chapter with an easy-to-use index that organizes art supplies, materials, and project names. Also included is an inspiring gallery of photos showing children at work creating art with action.

With these organizational formats and helpful details, the reader can easily flip through the pages and find an art activity suitable for the day, that is, one that suits materials on hand or time available.

What is the adult's role in *Action ART*?

Adults bringing *Action ART* activities to children's creative learning should think of themselves as guides and facilitators. Whoever you are – teacher, parent, child-care provider, librarian, big brother or sister, grandparent – adults have the job of gathering materials, setting up the art area, providing and assisting with a drying area, and in general, helping children to be comfortable and ready to create.

Some adults will need to let go of their ideas of how the finished product will turn out or exactly how the process will work – the process is key to children's success at trusting their own creativity, ideas, and thinking. That can be more difficult than it sounds, so be ready to remember who is creating and who is making the decisions for the outcome of the art. The child! One way to satisfy this challenge is to make some art yourself. You may discover how it feels to explore and create without an adult telling you what to make or how to do it, and not judging the outcome.

We tend to believe that children like praise for their artwork, but what they really need is "interaction." Instead of saying, "Good job!" or "Beautiful!" say, "Tell me about the colors you used," or "How did you make this curly paper stand up so tall?" Engage the child in conversation about his or her artwork.

Is *Action ART* messy?

Yes, art can be messy — and sometimes messier than you might like. Not all the projects in *Action ART* are messy. In fact, many are not messy at all! If mess makes you uncomfortable, be honest with your artists and ask for their help, both in controlling the mess and in cleaning up afterward. Try to build up your tolerance; start with something less messy and see how much your children enjoy it. Next time try something with a little more messy factor. Some days, when you know your own tolerance is low, choose a favorite tidy action art activity. And remember, artists like repeating the same project over and over because they get different results each time along with refining their skills.

To protect your space, it can help to move a project outdoors. It's important to simply be extra-prepared with damp sponges on hand for wiping messy fingers or a plastic shower curtain under the art paper to catch spills. The art activity pages offer hints and ideas for happy art experiences easy to cleanup.

You may find that some of your artists may decide to take their art process in another direction altogether. There's nothing wrong with that; in fact, it should be applauded! This means the artists are truly thinking about what they're doing, taking risks, and trying to make their own ideas come alive (you know, like real artists do!). Art encourages children to think, developing skills and confidence as they go.

What's special about *Action ART*?

If there needs to be only one reason to explore action art, it would have to simply be the fun of making art. Children learn by doing, and if they enjoy the doing, they will learn. Oh how they will learn! When children are involved in active art experiences, they will have fun, experience delight, be surprised, see beauty, see humor, and most of all, feel the unbridled sense of awe and joy and what it means to create one's own unique art.

When some children were asked about why they liked the art projects in *Action ART*, their replies were open and honest and inspiring. Here are a few quotes to enjoy, and to think about:

> • I liked finding out that paint does more things than I thought it did.

> • I got to use the biggest paper I ever saw, and I filled it with my art from one corner to the other corner, I mean, to all the corners.

> • Did you see my wire sculpture that moves in the wind? I made it really strong.

> • My friend and I worked and worked to make a collage. We used the teacher's spinner tray. I used lids from water bottles and he used cotton balls. We took turns and we had fun. Then we added glitter.

Action ART utilizes unusual techniques, unusual tools, and unexpected results. Translation? Unusual fun! If you are surprised by some of these art activities, imagine the surprise children will experience when they create with and explore them one by one.

Action ART – all things considered:

• Consider whether you'll be working with one child, a small group, or a large group. You will need to collect more materials or have more space for large groups.

• If you have a range of ages, consider that the time children will spend creating, their use of materials, and their own expectations will vary widely.

• There's no right way or wrong way for these art projects to turn out and not one single way to accomplish them. Be ready for individual thinking and outcomes.

• If you don't have all the materials listed for a project, consider substituting materials you do have. As adults, we need to be creative in how we make use of our on-hand materials and enjoy how this can change art explorations in a good way!

• The art projects in each chapter of *Action ART* progress from easiest to more complicated. Consider starting at the beginning of a chapter for an introductory art project and jumping to the end of a chapter to find a challenging art project.

• Consider that children learn by doing, and by doing, they learn to think and trust their own ideas. Process art builds confident independent adults who will take risks and find new ways to do things.

Action ART Icon Guide

Experience, Prep & Plan, and Art Technique Icons

Icons are positioned in the upper right corner of each activity's right-hand page. Icons help the reader – parents, teachers, or young artists – evaluate the attributes of an activity and help make choosing activities faster, easier, and perfectly matched to suit each child's creative interests and needs.

 Keep an eye out for the little bug who will tell true stories and share helpful opinions.

Child Experience

Age and skill do not always go hand in hand, so the **Child Experience Icons** indicate levels considered easiest, moderate, or most involved. All ages may explore any activity if supervised.

 EASIEST
One Star for beginning artists with little experience.

INTERMEDIATE
Two Stars for artists with some experience and moderate skill.

 CHALLENGING
Three Stars for more experienced artists. Adult assistance sometimes needed.

Adult Prep & Plan

Adult Prep & Plan Icons indicate the degree of involvement and planning time expected for the adult in charge, ranging from quick, to moderate, to significant.

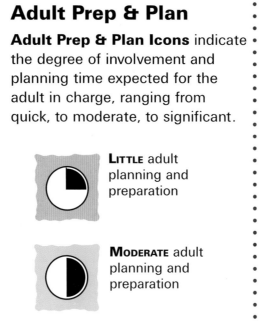

LITTLE adult planning and preparation

MODERATE adult planning and preparation

 Involved adult planning and preparation

Art Techniques

The **Art Technique Icons** help the reader quickly determine the key material or art technique needed for the process art activity. When multiple techniques are used, the secondary technique will be listed in a second box.

PAINT   DRAW   COLLAGE   MIXTURE

TAPE   CUT   PRINT   SCULPT

CHALK   CLAY OR DOUGH   BY HAND   MESSY ALERT

 *Action ART* © 2015 Bright Ring Publishing

Table of Contents

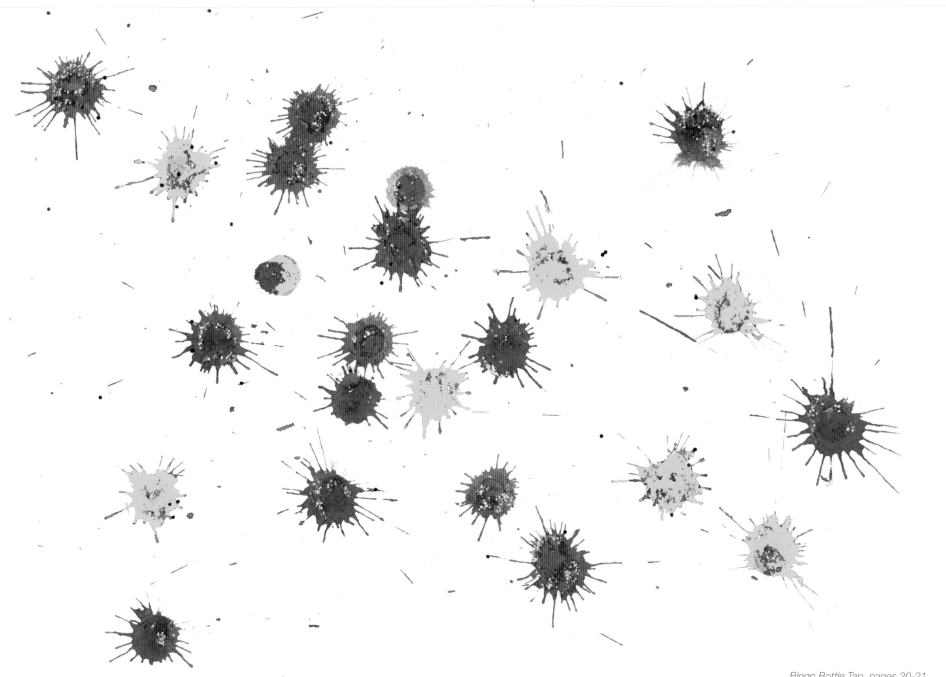

1 Smacking Squeezing Tapping

Hammering Tees

Hammering golf tees into a foam block is a delightfully non-messy action art technique enjoyed by all ages and abilities. One big block works well for either a small group sculpture or an individual sculpture. Adding individually selected collage materials will make the hammered sculpture unique to each artist.

A first session of practice without collage materials was a good introduction for three-year-old artists who hammered golf tees into a foam block. Later, more collage materials were offered to extend the activity. The trend that day was hammering tees through objects directly into the foam. ~ MAK

Golf tees are easily pounded into a foam block to create a flexible and colorful sculpture with many options for adding collage materials.

Materials

- Golf tees, variety of colors, in a low-sided container or bowl
- Hammer, mallet, or toy mallet from pounding toy
- Block of packing foam (from shipping computers, appliances, or other products)
- Scissors and glue, optional
- Choice of collage materials spread out in a tray or box with low-hsides. Some suggestions are –

Beads	Paper scraps
Bottle caps	Pipe cleaners
Buttons	Ribbons
Cotton balls	Scraps of art tissue
Faux flowers	Small pinecones
Gems	Stickers
Leaves, supple	Yarn

Cover the block with fabric or paper, and the base block becomes an all new art experience.

Tees photography by Mrs. O'Connor
learnthroughplayslc.blogspot.com

Action Process

1. Arrange all the materials on the workspace in easy reach for either an individual, for partners, or for a small group.

2. Pounding the Golf Tee: To insert a golf tee in the foam block, hold the tee in the non-drawing hand pincer fingers, just below the flat head of the tee. Carefully pound the tee into the foam block with a hammer or mallet with the drawing hand. Another technique is to push the tee into the block by hand until it stands on its own, and then hammer the rest of it into the block. Some artists like to hammer it all the way in, and others like to leave the tee sticking out of the block.

3. Continue hammering golf tees into the foam block in any design or arrangement, many or few, tall or short, all over the top and even the sides of the block.

4. Once the desired number of tees is complete, collage items may be added to the sculpture. Some ideas:
   • Glue single items on the head of each golf tee,
   or tie ribbons or yarn from one tee to another.
   • Push another golf tee through a scrap of paper and then pound in the tee, pinning the paper in place.

Alternative materials for a hammering sculpture are effective, like this round pumpkin. Just imagine the fragrance that will fill the art area.

~ Suggestion ~

Repeat art activities often
to build skills, techniques,
and confidence.

More Ideas to Explore

Cover the foam with one of the following paper ideas, and then hammer in the tees. Add collage items:

• painting or drawing
• colorful wrapping paper, aluminum foil or foil paper, colorful art tissue paper
• other paper, including: doilies, cupcake papers, used greeting cards

Art Hockey

Chopsticks work like hockey sticks and marbles work like pucks for this very active art experience using quick action, movement, and genuine laughter.

At one time, my preschool boys would have declared this hockey activity "boys-only"! Things have definitely changed! Now it's art for everyone together, with everyone playing and laughing as they smack a marble flying back and forth through paint.   ~ BBZ

Two friends create a hockey-style artwork with marbles and chopsticks. Look at the blur of their movement! The finished art to the right is a story map of their creative process and active involvement.

Materials

- Big box with sides cut to about 2″–3″ high
- Paper to fit the bottom of the box
- Tempera paints, choices of colors
- Bowls or containers, one for each color of paint
- Marbles, 2–3 for each color, and spoons
- Chopstick "hockey sticks" (choose from spoons, dowels, straws, or other sticks), one per artist
- Two artists

Action Process

1. Set the box on a low table or on the floor. Place a sheet of paper in the bottom of the box. Artists stand or kneel on either side of the box.

2. Pour about an inch of paint in the bowls. Place two to three marbles in each bowl.

3. Spoon a paint-dipped marble onto the paper.

4. One of the artists begins the action by smacking the marble across the paper and the two continue smacking the marble back and forth until they need more paint.

5. Change marbles and colors whenever artists say they are ready.

Hockey photography Barbara Zaborowski © Bright Ring Publishing 2014

More Ideas to Explore

- Try two or three marbles in the box simultaneously.
- Try golf balls, rubber balls, spiky balls, or ping pong balls. Stronger "hockey sticks" will be needed, like spatulas or kitchen spoons.
- One artist can play Art Hockey alone on a tray or in a box.

Wood Block Smack 'n' Tap

Two choices of art ideas with wooden blocks make these press-and-print activities twice the fun! Artists will think of even more wood printing techniques, guaranteed!

Materials

- Wood block, approximately 4" square by 1" thick
- Tempera paints in cups, with spoons and paintbrushes
- Construction paper, any colors or size
- Rags or old towel, optional

The artist to the left spends a focused exploratory time mixing colors for her wood block print.

Below: Creativity often involves many steps: mixing, painting, pressing, lifting, and pressing again.

Richard is often hard to please with art activities, but when wood is involved, he's 100% on board. His favorites are sanding, hammering, and working with nuts and bolts. To quote Richard, "You gotta know how to use wood, Mrs. Kohl. There's a lot to know." And Richard is right about that!   ~ MAK

Wood Block photography Zannifer Rolich, UNR (University of Nevada Reno) Child Care, 2014

Action ART © 2015 Bright Ring Publishing

Action Process

1. Use a paintbrush or a spoon to dribble and drop a few blobs of paint on the flat surface of the block, not too thick and not too thin (about as thick as a quarter). Some artists cover their blocks with paint, and other artists use less paint. Both ways work.

2. Ready for the action? Gently turn the block over and press it very firmly on paper. Do not wiggle the block. Just press firmly down and press hard, holding briefly.

3. When ready, lift the block and see the print on the paper. Hint: Peeling the paper from the block may be necessary.

Add more paint and make more prints!
Suggestions:
  - Overlap a dry print with a new fresh print.
  - See how paint colors look on different colors of paper.

Hint: The block may be washed in the sink and dried with rags or paper towels, and then used again.

More Ideas to Explore

• Glue cardboard shapes on the wooden block, press in paint, and then press on paper to make prints.

• Dribble paint on a sheet of paper and cover lightly with a second sheet of paper. Press the block firmly on the paper, moving the block to a new area and pressing each time. Then peel the papers apart to see the action revealed.

This young artist prefers to drop his block to make a print.

Bingo Bottle Tap

Bingo bottles filled with liquid watercolors make cheerful paint splots with splashes radiating out from the centers. Use one color, or try many colors all on one paper.

Materials

- Bingo bottles (small sponge-tip plastic bottles), one for each color
- Liquid watercolors
- White paper or construction paper in lighter colors (try a variety of papers: paper plates, white tissue paper, paper towels, watercolor painting paper, newsprint)

Reminder: Most artists need more than one piece of paper with which to experiment and test their painting techniques and ideas.

We found pre-filled bingo bottles at the dollar store, which we have refilled many many times! We work with multiple ages, and this art experience works well for all ages together. Bingo bottles are less messy than some painting activities – nice when you need a break.
~ MAK

Bingo bottle photography Margaret Mahowald, Calvary Child-care Center, Calvary Lutheran Church, Golden Valley, MN. CALVARY.ORG

Action ART © 2015 Bright Ring Publishing

Action Process

1. Fill each bingo bottle about 1/3 full with one color choice of liquid watercolors.

   Hint: Paint may be thinned to make liquid watercolors last longer. Simply add a little water to each bottle.

2. Turn the bingo bottle upside down and lightly tap, smash, dab, smoosh, or press it on the paper. Experiment to create splash and splot designs with radiating color spikes coming off from the center.

   Note: Some artists like to practice techniques on scrap paper, while still others like to jump right in! To get the idea, artists can practice making splots with bingo bottles and clear water, tapping them on colored paper.

3. Explore making splots with light pressure and with heavy pressure. Other techniques like dragging or pushing will give unique results.

4. Try overlapping dots or colors. Add a little glitter to wet paint if you like, and you won't even need glue. Glitter glue is also a nice touch.

A first bingo bottle experience! This artist begins slowly with green, and then expands his experience to mixing colors and shapes.

- No bingo bottles? No worries! Try one of these ideas:

  – Cut a kitchen sponge into several little cubes and attach a pinching clothespin to each cube as a handle.

  – Roll a damp sponge cube and push it tightly into the top of any small bottle. (See an example to the left.)

More Ideas to Explore

- When the painting is dry, trace around shapes and colors with a permanent or water-based maker. Artists who look closely will see many surprise designs hidden within the splots.
- Multi-Bingo Bottles: Try two-handed painting with a bingo bottle in each hand. Next try two bottles in each hand. Would someone like to try even more?

Tube-a-Roo

Smacking paint splots with a paper towel tube or other smacking tool has impressive results that all ages enjoy. Try it, you'll see! Explore with a big smack and a light smack to experiment with the variety of design possibilities.

I taught a preschool group including a little boy who would never choose to do art. Never. He was usually building with LEGOs or blocks, also creative. This active art activity appealed to him, and he forsook his beloved blocks to try it. The great thing was that once he'd tried, he revisited the art table again and again to try other activities.   ~ BBZ

Some artists choose to paint the tube first, and then slap it on paper. Others choose to spoon puddles of paint on the paper and then slap the puddles. Expect vigorous slapping and spatters!

Cardboard tube photography Barbara Zaborowski ©
Bright Ring Publishing 2014

Materials

- Tempera paints, several colors
- Small containers or paper cups, one for each color
- Plastic spoons, one for each color
- Large sheet of paper (newsprint, butcher paper, craft paper, back of a used poster)
- Paper towel tubes

Action Process

1. Spread a sheet of paper on the workspace. Pour tempera paints into small cups. Place a spoon by each cup on the workspace. Place the paper towel tubes on the workspace too.
2. Spoon a small puddle or splot of paint on the paper.
3. Pick up the paper towel tube and "smack" the splot with the tube. A hard action smack will spread the paint out more and may even cause a considerable splash! A gentle smack will simply press the paint into a wider shape. Consider other motions to explore, like rolling, poking, and twisting.
4. Add another paint splot and repeat the smacking action. Keep adding splots and smacking each one. The paint will spread in different ways.
5. Explore techniques, pressures, action, energy, and tools.

More Ideas to Explore

- Try all kinds of smacking tools: flyswatter, pool noodles, hands, feet, block of wood, sock filled with rice or sand, spatula. Look around the art corner, garage, or kitchen for more utensils or tools that might be interesting to try. The photos to the right show Spatula Smacking.
- Soak a small sponge with thinned paint. Place it on large paper. Then WHAP the sponge with a smacking tool to make splashy designs.
- Dip a smacking tool in a pan of paint. Smack the paper with the tool. Overlap prints and mix colors in any way. Splash warning!
- Fill knee-high socks with sand and tie off. Swing and splat!

Kitchen utensils are perfect tools for exploring the paint-smacking technique on paper.

Spatula photography @ 2014 Amanda Sipple, messyhandslessonplans.com

Squeezy Sponges

Squeezing paint from a sponge involves feeling paint on one's hands and using paint in new ways. This activity can involve a lot of paint, so begin with small amounts. You can always add more.

Artists often take great pride in their bravery to be messy and creative.

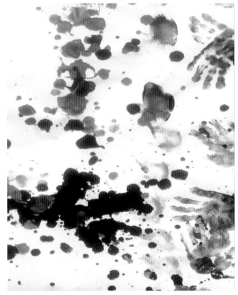

I thought squeezing paint from sponges might sound like a whole lot more fun than it would turn out to be. I was so wrong! We ended up making a giant mural that almost everyone worked on. And two boys didn't want to quit, even as our morning wore down.   ~ BBZ

Materials

- Tarp or protected surface
- Large pieces of paper
- Tempera or washable paints
- Bowls or shallow containers
- Kitchen sponges, or larger sponges cut down for artist use
- Water in a bucket or tub
- Old towels, rags, or paper towels

Action Process

1. Set paint, tarps or other protection, and sheets of paper out ready to use. Pour a little paint in shallow bowls or containers. Use as many colors as you like, one bowl for each color. Begin with less paint, and add more as needed.

2. Sponges must be moist to begin. Soak sponges in water and squeeze out as much as possible to keep sponges from instantly absorbing all the paint. Artists like to help.

3. Ready for action? Dip a damp sponge in a bowl of paint. Some children will dip one color per sponge, while others will mix several colors per sponge. This is normal and is one of the reasons that starting with less paint helps keep colors fresh.

4. Squeeze the paint out of a sponge over the paper. Artists can move the squeezing effect slowly over the paper, or stay in one place and watch the paint landing. Some artists will want to print with the sponges or make handprints, while others will want to stand and squeeze with the joy of exploring a new technique. Both are welcome and honored techniques.

5. Allow the paintings to dry. The thickness of the paint squeezing may require overnight drying. Some artists will want to save their explorations, while others will only remember the process.

Sponge photography
Barbara Zaborowski
© Bright Ring Publishing 2014

More Ideas to Explore

- Once artists have tried the squeezing technique, bring out additional painting tools, such as, eye-droppers, pipettes, spoons, or Q-tips (cotton buds). Combine the use of different tools to see different effects.
- Press a damp sponge into paint, and press it gently on paper to make a sponge print. Slapping a painty sponge on paper is another action-filled art activity to explore.

Slap Glove Paint

This surprising and enjoyable art activity of slapping paint-covered rubber gloves on paper is a favorite. Fill the gloves, for stability, with sand, rice, or dry beans; then dip in paint, and WHAP on paper! Painting in new ways stirs the desire to create and explore.

Materials

- Paper, any kind (large newsprint works well)
- Rubber gloves, one for each color (dishwashing gloves, latex cooking gloves or medical gloves)
- Dry beans to fill the gloves (or rice, sand, crumbled paper, or other materials to give the gloves heft)
- Tempera paints, several colors of choice
- Paper plates or other flat container, one for each color
- Tape, optional, to stabilize
- Yarn, for tying off gloves

Yesterday, this activity was full of noisy-glove slapping and even more noisy laughter. However, one girl chose to place the painted gloves carefully on her paper, creating art with her own specific process. Meanwhile, all around her was the chaos of exuberant smacking, which didn't bother her as she continued with her own art idea.   ~ BBZ

Glove photography Barbara Zaborowski © Bright Ring Publishing 2014

Action Process

1. Set up the art table for painting with protection and paper. Fill the rubber gloves with beans, crumbled paper, cotton balls, or another material you have on hand. Slightly heavy materials give the gloves heft and control, but any materials are fun to experiment with. Then tie off the wrists of the gloves with yarn, giving several wraps and pulling tightly.

2. Pour a different color puddle of paint on each paper plate Place a filled-and-tied rubber glove on each plate.

3. Ready for the action? Pick up the glove, prepare to slap, and whap! Slap it on the newsprint. What a pattern it makes!

4. Repeat the action. Repaint the glove as needed and keep slapping designs. Note: Don't be surprised if some artists experiment to see what other movements might make interesting paint designs, including: dragging, pushing, twirling, and pressing. (Artists have many experimental ideas for this activity!)

5. Change gloves to slap paint with different colors.

6. Repeat until satisfied with the painting. Want more? Bring out fresh paper, and slap-paint a new painting. Artists often want more than one turn before they are ready to move on.

A painted blue glove is carefully pressed into the design just below the red.

More Ideas to Explore

*   Fill each glove with a different material and experience how weight influences design and slap-power.
*   Group: Cover a table with a large sheet of paper taped down, and set out at least one glove for each artist. Trade colors or gloves anytime. Everyone slap-paints together!
*   Let's talk slap-painting! Use words to encourage or define designs, like "rub, tap, slide, dance, skate, hop, or fly!"

Big Time Dabbing

Cut several large holes in a sheet of cardboard, and use these as a stencil type template for big action-dabbing with large brushes and tempera paints.

 These brothers were excited to explore big brushes and big paper. The holes cut in the template sheet were drawn by the boys and cut by their adventurous mama. All painting was done by the boys on their own. Working outside made cleanup a breeze! Maybe they can try this with smaller brushes and smaller paper – "mini dabbing."   ~ MAK

Dabbing photography @ Sarah Valeos 2014, www.sarahvaleos.com

The important learning for these two brothers was the process of creating and discovering how unusual art materials behave. The final product was the result of exploration and learning, not their goal.

Materials

- Sheet of cardboard or poster board
- Crayon or marker
- Strong scissors
- House-painting brushes or large brushes (sponge brushes work well)
- Tempera paints
- Bucket of clear water for rinsing, and an old towel or rags
- Containers for paint, one for each color (half-gallon milk cartons, washed and cut down to 4"–6" tall, work well)
- Large paper: butcher paper or craft paper on a roll
- Shipping tape or duct tape, or rocks
- Work area: wall, floor, or ground

Action Process

1. Tape the large paper to a work wall, or stretch it out on the ground. Secure with tape or rocks. Fill containers halfway or less with tempera paint, one container for each color.

2. Draw some big shapes on the sheet of cardboard. An adult can cut the holes; cardboard is difficult for kids to cut. Holes may be abstract and ragged, or precisely planned shapes. Then tape or secure the cardboard over the paper.

3. Now for the action! Dip a large house-painting brush or sponge brush into paint. Then vigorously dab the brush in the holes of the cardboard and the paper showing through the holes. Change colors as desired. Note: The brush may be rinsed in the bucket at any time, and squeezed dry with the towel or rags.

4. Keep dabbing until all the holes have been painted in. Note: Some artists want to paint the entire cardboard, and this is fine. Others want to move the template around so more holes can be painted.

5. Let the paint dry slightly, and then remove tape or rocks holding the cardboard. Pull the cardboard away to see the dabbed designs left on the large paper.

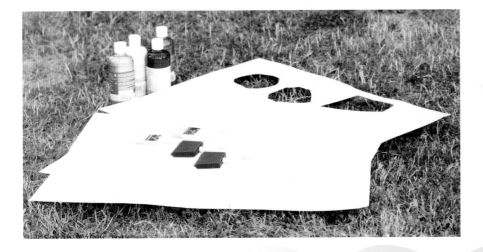

More Ideas to Explore

- Artists like to fill in the unpainted areas of the paper, which they can do with any favorite art technique. Consider more paint, markers, collage, or cutting holes in the paper.
- To further decorate the paper, fill misting spray bottles with water and lightly spray the paint designs.
- Lightly spray the art with thinned liquid watercolors from a misting spray bottle.

Squeeze Spray Tissue

A handheld spray bottle is the tool that makes these two art tissue activities come to life. Be sure to use "bleeding" art tissue or craft tissue paper, and not generic gift-wrap tissue paper.

Materials

- Handheld spray bottles or misting bottles filled with water
- Bleeding art tissue paper: scraps, shapes, or full sheets
  Note: Crepe paper is a substitute for bleeding art tissue paper.
- Easel
- Drawing paper
- Watercolor paper
- Cup of water and small paintbrush
- Scissors, optional
- Grocery trays or other containers to sort and hold the tissue pieces
- Paper towels

Easel photograph @ 2014 Gretchen Morgan

Four-year-old Risa (not shown) loves art time and puts a lot of thought into creating. She is delicate and careful at the easel to press her tissue scraps onto the wet paper. She pats gently, stands back, and tilts her head this way and that. She carefully adds one more piece overlapping the other. Watching her is like seeing a great master working out the next great masterpiece.   ~ MAK

Action Process 1

Easel Spray Tissue

1. Clip a sheet of paper to the easel. Drawing paper works better than newsprint.

2. Spray a little water on the paper.

3. Stick any shapes or scraps of art tissue on the wet paper.

4. Now spray again to soak the art tissue. It will run and blur. Use a paintbrush, if you like, to spread the colors.

5. Add more tissue scraps. The colors will start to mix.

6. The tissue will hold without glue. Dry completely when done.

Tissue photography on orange table Barbara Zaborowski © Bright Ring Publishing 2014

Action Process 2
Tissue Stain

1. Place a sheet of drawing paper on the workspace.

2. Arrange art tissue scraps, shapes, or pieces on the drawing paper in any design or arrangement. No water or glue is needed at this point.

3. Lightly spray the tissue art so that it begins to soak and stick to the paper.

4. Pat the tissue gently with fingers to flatten and encourage colors to bleed.

5. Remove and peel away the tissue pieces. A stain print will be left on the paper. Gently blot extra water with a paper towel.

6. Wash hands with warm soapy water to remove color from fingers.

More Ideas to Explore

- Run water over a sheet of watercolor paper; pat the paper on the table to flatten and stick to the table. Press tissue pieces into the damp watercolor paper. The paper will absorb color. Choose to peel away the tissue, or leave in place.

- Scrunch up balls of art tissue scraps and place in shallow cups, add a little water, and use as watercolor paints.

This artist chose to leave her tissue pieces in place to dry with their beautiful torn edges and overlapping colors.

Pounding Paint

Tapping paint-filled paper plates with a hammer creates great patterns! For a cleaner way to hammer on paint, "pound paint" with a bedsheet or shower curtain controlling the spatters. Reluctant artists? Not when you bring out the hammers!

My artists had experienced pounding paint on a white sheet and drawing on a plastic shower curtain. We combined the two activities! They pounded paint on a clear shower curtain! We entered it in a kids' art show. Our shower curtain art (cut into long strips and hanging from a rod) was accepted at a theater in downtown Phoenix where it hung under a sign that said,

HAVE YOU EVER WALKED THROUGH A PIECE OF ART?

~ BBZ

Materials

- Bedsheet, tablecloth, or shower curtain
- Paper plates
- Paints (tempera paints for fabric, acrylic paints for plastic)
- Rubber mallet or hammer (mallet is quieter)
- Tarp or plastic tablecloth for protection

Pounding paint photography Barbara Zaborowski © Bright Ring Publishing 2014

Action Process

1. Spread out a tarp on the ground. Spread a bedsheet on top of the tarp. (If using a plastic shower curtain instead of a sheet, do the same.)

2. Put two or three colors of paint blobs in the middle of a paper plate.

3. Slide the paper plate UNDERNEATH the bedsheet. The further into the middle of the sheet the plate is placed, the less mess will result. (When the plate is near the edges of the sheet, watch out for splashes of paint from beneath.)

4. Now for the action, and be prepared to see energetic involvement! Pound the plate from outside the sheet with the mallet or hammer. The paint will spread in all directions underneath the sheet. Pound the areas of spreading paint, too. (Hint: For younger painters, try using plastic or wooden mallets typical with pounding toys.)

5. Repeat steps 1 through 3 until the entire sheet is covered to the artist's or group's satisfaction. The results will vary depending on the hammer choice, the technique of artists, and the amount of paint used.

6. The sheet will be heavily decorated with paint and can be used to cover a wall or used as a curtain. Read More Ideas to Explore for variations.

Pounding on paint puddles placed on paper plates under an old bedsheet offers an element of surprise young artists appreciate.

More Ideas to Explore

- If you're painting something you intend to use, like shirts or a tablecloth, acrylic paints can be mixed 50/50 with fabric medium (or textile medium) available from craft stores. When dry, either iron the item or dry it in the dryer to "fix" the paint. It is then washable.
- Create as an inviting display for an art show or event.

Spinning Hanging CDs, pages 38-39
Far left CD image Ronda Harbaugh 2014
Middle and right CD images Gill Robertson 2014

2 Rolling
Spinning
Swinging

Rolling Bubble Wrap

Assign a rolling pin to the art box because it will have many artsy uses, including covering it with Bubble Wrap to make rolling prints.

Materials

- Rolling pin
- Bubble Wrap (Note: Most artists want to press hard enough to pop the bubbles.)
- Tape
- Butcher paper or other paper
- Tray with edges
- Tempera paints, variety of colors
- Spoon or brush

 This artist cheerfully jumped into the discovery of Bubble Wrap rolled in paint, but before long, he had an idea to include his favorite toy train to add tracks. As his work progressed, he experimented with a hose and water. Young artists often have their own tests and methods to explore.
~ MAK

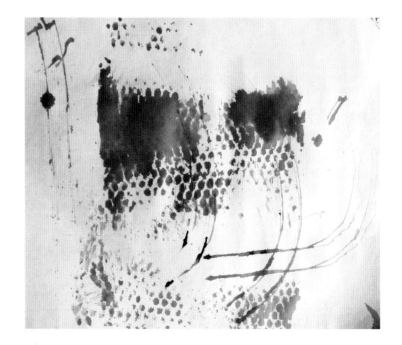

Action ART © 2015 Bright Ring Publishing

Action Process

1. Cover the workspace with paper so there is enough room for rolling and printing. Tape paper down so it won't wiggle or lift.

2. Cover the rolling pin with a square of Bubble Wrap and a little tape to hold.

3. Pour puddles of paint on the tray. Pour as many colors as you wish. One color is good for beginners.

4. Roll the bubble-wrapped rolling pin through the paint, covering the Bubble Wrap, and then roll it on the paper. Roll and roll until the color wears out.

5. Then roll the bubble-wrapped rolling pin in paint again, and back to the paper to roll more designs. Add more paint to the tray as needed.

From rolling pins, to toy trains, and ultimately to a hose and water, this young artist freely embraces his unique exploration of Bubble Wrap.

Bubble roll photography © 2014 MaryAnn F. Kohl, courtesy of Carey Lamothe

More Ideas to Explore

- Create handprints with "Bubble Wrap mittens."
- Create prints with Bubble Wrap arms, elbows, knees, head, fingers, and more.
- Tape Bubble Wrap to the workspace. Paint the bubbles with tempera paints. Press a piece of paper on the Bubble Wrap to lift a bubbly print.

Spinning Hanging CDs

If you have used CDs, recycle them and create spinning designs that are surprisingly beautiful. Bring out the permanent markers (the more colors the better). The action is in the spin, and the art is in the design. Together they are "Action Art!"

Materials

- CDs, recycled
- Permanent markers
- Fishing line, hook, or tape for hanging CD
- Scissors

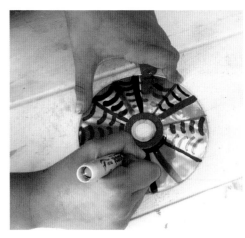

When one little preschool artist discovered drawing on silvery CDs with permanent markers, he became entranced with complicated designs and color mixing. When he hung his work in the sunshine in the "forest," he said, "That's my shine-art!"   ~ MAK

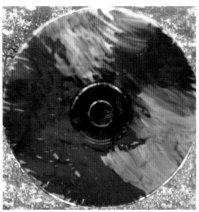

Above: CD photograph Ronda Harbaugh 2014   *All other CD photography Gill Robertson 2014, Teddy Bear Daycare, Souris, Manitoba, Canada*

Action Process

1. With permanent markers, like Sharpies, draw designs directly on the shiny CDs. Draw on both sides.

2. When designs are done, loop fishing line through the hole in the center of the CD (or use other strong thread) and tie a knot. Hang the CD from a hook or with tape from the ceiling, in a window, in a tree, or from a doorjamb.
   Hint: Hanging a series of CDs from a clothes hanger of piece of wood makes a colorful mobile.

Manitoba, Canada

3. Design more CDs and hang them together or spaced all around the room or outdoors. Natural air currents will spin the CDs 'round and 'round, showing a mixture of colors and designs, often reflecting light that dances wherever the reflections land.
   Note: To see the colors spin more dramatically, spin the CD by hand. It will windup tight, and then unwind on its own.

More Ideas to Explore

- **Spinning Top CD**: Trace the CD on drawing paper and cut out the circle. Draw on the paper circle. Then glue the circle to one side of the CD (just a few dots of glue will do). Glue a water bottle cap over the hole on the top side of the CD. Glue a large marble over the hole on the blank underside. Hold the bottle cap between pointer and thumb, and spin the CD on the marble.

- Draw designs on a clear plastic lid (which can also fly like a Frisbee).

The individually designed CDs were hung in the garden to spin with the summer breezes.

Lazy Susan Collage

Spinning a plastic "lazy Susan" turntable from the kitchen facilitates art action when a collage takes shape. Choosing collage items is half the fun! Artists will wonder which collage items spin best: lightweight, heavy, or both?

Materials

- Lazy Susan, flat plastic turntable (spinner)
- Large paper (craft paper, butcher paper, back of old poster, poster board)
- White glue in squeeze bottle (other glue, tape, or stapler come in handy)
  Hint: Glue will need to dry for ten minutes or so before the paper can be lifted without pieces falling off.
- Choice of collage materials.
  Some suggestions are -

Beads	Pebbles
Buttons	Pinecones
Cotton balls	Pipe cleaner pieces
Feathers	Pom-poms
Foam shapes	Pony beads
Paper scraps	Popsicle sticks
Paper clips	Wood scraps, shavings

Both Piper and Finne agree that practicing spinning the turntable better prepared them for the real art experience. They say they found that spinning fewer items at a time spread out the design best. Piper says that if there is an area of the collage that is still empty, try spinning in the opposite direction.
~ JG

Spin photography 2014 Jennifer Grahame

Action ART © 2015 Bright Ring Publishing

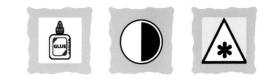

Action Process

1. Practice spinning the spinner by hand. There are many techniques, such as holding the edge, pressing the pointer finger on the flat space and pushing it around, or using two hands and crossing over to keep it going. The artist can decide which technique works best to get a good spin. Any spin is a good spin!

2. Place the spinner in the middle of the paper. Select one type of collage item, like buttons, and place a handful on the spinner.

3. Ready for the action? Spin the spinner and watch the buttons fly onto the paper! Glue them in place with a dot of glue.

4. Try another collage material. Will heavy items spin better than light? Or will light items spin best? Spin the spinner with a choice of collage materials, and let the items land where they will. Glue now or glue later; either way is fine.

5. Continue to spin collage materials out from the spinner and onto the paper. Once a good selection has been spun onto the paper, and the artist is satisfied, proceed to glue any loose pieces in place. (Sometimes tape or a stapler can help too.)

Finne and Piper show how sisters work together to create art.

More Ideas to Explore

- The spinner will leave an empty area on the paper when it is removed. Fill in with more art of choice. Color it in, draw in, glue in colored paper or foil, photocopy of the artist's face, or other art ideas. Leaving it blank is fine too.

- Instead of paper, spread contact paper, sticky side up, on the workspace. When items spin out from the spinner, press them into the sticky surface where they land.

Twisty CDs & Plates

Twisting paint-covered CDs or paper plates into circle art calls for exuberant color combinations and freedom of exploration. Use big arm action or just a little. Every design is a burst of mixed color surprise.

Materials

- Tempera paints (not too thin or runny), or other paints, in squirt bottles (No squirt bottles? "Spoon" puddles of paint.)
- Paper plates or used CDs (compact discs)
- Poster board or big paper for CD Twisty
- Water and old towel (Hint: To reuse or clean CDs, wipe or rinse in warm water and dry.)

Action Process One

Paper Plate Twisty

1. Squirt or spoon paint onto the back of a paper plate.
2. Place a second plate over the painted plate, and twist the plates back and forth together. Then lift the plate to see the circle art on both plates. (Some artists like to further twist the plates on a larger poster board or butcher paper.)

We learned about the great master Wassily Kandinsky's work through the art docent program, and had made circle-art in his style. Now, months later, one artist surprised me when she looked at her Twisty CD art and said, "Look, I made a Kandinsky!"   ~ MAK

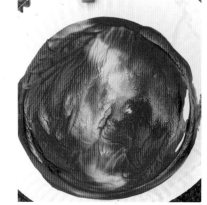

Paper plate photography above: Barbara Zaborowski Barbara Zaborowski © Bright Ring Publishing 2014

Action Process Two

CD Twisty

1. Place a poster board or large paper on the workspace. Fill squirt bottles with tempera paints. Squirt some blobs of paint on a CD.

2. Turn the CD over and onto the big paper or poster board. With one hand fully spread out on the CD, push down and twist the CD back and forth to spread the color. Then lift the CD to see the circle art on the paper.

3. Quickly rinse and dry the CD, or use another CD that is ready to go. Repeat the paint and twisting, changing color combinations in any way.
Note: Some artists like to line the circles up next to each other. Other artists like a more random effect, sometimes even overlapping one circle over another.

The design possibilities are endless! If you don't have CDs, you can use jar lids or cardboard circles or the bottom of a saucepan! Every circle material offers a different experience, discovery, and art skill.

Twisty CD photographs above: Roopa Shri, author of Putti's World blog

CD dot photo above: Tammy Oveson, M.Ed., Learn 'n Play Preschool, Waite Park, MN

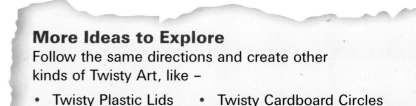

More Ideas to Explore
Follow the same directions and create other kinds of Twisty Art, like –

- Twisty Plastic Lids
- Twisty Jar Lids
- Twisty Frisbees
- Twisty Cardboard Circles
- Twisty Quarters
- Twisty Dinner Plates

Wet Tissue Roll

Art tissue, called **"bleeding tissue,"** comes in many bright colors that are easily released with moisture. Add a spray bottle of water to moisten and a rolling pin to press. Let the rolling pin squeeze colors and designs into action!

"Mrs. Kohl, I'm making painty pie!"

"I see you rolling something. Are you rolling your pie?"

"Yes. My pie is a painty pie. I'm making it for you."

"Mm-mm, thank you. I think you are an art-baker today!"

"I make pie every day at my house."

~ MAK

Materials

- Squares or scraps of bleeding art tissue paper or crepe paper from party decorations (Note: gift-wrap tissue will not work.)
- Scissors
- Spray bottle filled with water, and water in a cup with a paintbrush
- White paper
- Rolling pin for art use (not cooking)
- Damp sponge for quick cleanup

Action ART © 2015 Bright Ring Publishing

Action Process

1. Select some squares or large scraps of art tissue paper (bleeding art tissue paper). Crepe paper torn into good-sized scraps will also work.

2. Scrunch some of the scraps into balls. Place a ball of tissue on the paper.

3. Spray the ball with water to moisten. To make the tissue extra-moist, drop some water on it from a paintbrush.

4. Next, roll the rolling pin over the wet ball of tissue to squeeze out the color and flatten the ball. Color will press out in interesting designs. Further roll the liquid that squeezes out into even more designs.
   Hint: A damp sponge on the table is a handy way to swipe fingers and hands to help keep mess under control.

5. Add more balls, more water, and more rolling. Tissue balls may be left on the paper, or peeled away, as the artist chooses.

6. Let the art dry. Meanwhile, wash hands with soap and water. (The color will come out the same day, or within a day or two.)

Tissue roll photography by Margaret Mahowald, Calvary Child-care Center, Calvary Lutheran Church, Golden Valley, MN. calvary.org

More Ideas to Explore
Cardboard Tube Variation

- Try the same basic moist tissue technique with a strong cardboard tube. Spoon puddles of tempera paint on the paper. Roll the tube like a rolling pin through the puddles, spreading and flattening the paint and creating designs. Some artists re-roll the tube in clean areas of the paper. Other artists paint directly on the tube, rolling it across a large sheet of paper or butcher paper.

Coffee Can Incline

Plunk paint-dipped marbles inside a coffee can lined with paper. Roll the can *up* an incline and see the surprise inside!

We've tried many variations of marble painting, but my favorite was the time a group of girls sat in a circle and rolled the can from one to another. They laughed so much that they forgot they had art in the can! Meanwhile, they became fast friends, and art was how they found each other.   ~ BBZ

The artist investigates the painting from her coffee can art and adds a little more design by hand.

The artists drops a marble into the coffee container, ready for incline rolling.

Materials

- Paper, cut to line a coffee can or other choice of cans
- Coffee can, Pringles can, or similar-sized cans with snap-on lids
- Scissors
- Tempera paints, several different colors
- Cups or small containers, one for each paint color
- Marbles, several for each paint color
- Spoons to handle marbles
- Incline (ideas: sturdy cardboard propped up on books, a paint easel board, or a piece of plywood on blocks at one end)
- Masking tape or other tape (optional)

Coffee can photography Barbara Zaborowski
© Bright Ring Publishing 2014

Action Process

1. Cut paper to fit inside the can. Place it in the can, being sure the paper covers all sides of the can.

2. Fill containers with 1"-2" of paint. Drop several marbles in each container.

3. With a spoon, remove two or three marbles and drop them into the paper-lined can. The marbles can come from different colors or be all the same. (Eventually try one color alone or several colors together to see the different results.)

4. Snap the top securely on the can (may tape for extra security).

5. Ready for the action? Sit on the floor or ground facing the incline. Roll the can up the incline and catch it as it rolls back. Repeat numerous times for fun and exploration.

6. Remove the paper and see the surprise results!

7. Insert a clean sheet of paper for more action and painting. (Some artists like to replace the same paper and add to it.) Repeat all steps. Explore with more marbles and different combinations of colors.

More Ideas to Explore

• Expand the action: kick, toss, or spin the can. (Photo to right.)
• Try the same with a cardboard box: kick, toss, spin, roll.
• Roll the marble-filled can back and forth to each other on the floor to create a partner or a group painting.
• Try other objects in the can, like golf balls, dry beans, or pebbles. (Photo right: pebbles have become painted in the process.)

Above: Rolling the can up the incline with paint and marbles inside.
Below: Kicking the can on the grass with paint and pebbles inside.

Kick photos Jamie Hand, 2014, Owner Hand Made Kids Art, handmadekidsart.com

Suspended Paint Brushing

Join with a partner to paint with paintbrushes suspended on rope over a large sheet of paper. Then work together to paint.

Two boys paint with suspended paintbrushes with the help of a friend who is manning the bowls of paint. This process takes teamwork!

The last time my class did this activity, there were two pairs of kids working: two girls who were close friends, chatting and giggling, and two boys who didn't know each other well. As the boys worked together, they negotiated, communicated, traded ideas, compromised, and took turns. I felt privileged to see the dawn of a friendship before my eyes.
~ BBZ

Suspended photography Barbara Zaborowski © Bright Ring Publishing 2014

Action Process

1. Spread out the tarp, tablecloth, or newspaper on the ground. Place a large sheet of paper on the cover. An adult can tie the paintbrushes onto the cord spaced about 6 inches apart. (A good number is two or three brushes per cord. Use one cord, or if you like, use two cords, one for each hand!)

2. A helper can dip the paintbrushes into paint colors that the artists select, each brush in a different color, while the two artists stand ready at each end of the rope.

3. Next, the two artists step back and slowly pull the cord taut over the paper.

4. These art partners will need to work together to move the brushes across the paper. Younger artists usually don't keep the cord taut and simply drag the brushes around on the paper. This is fine, and gives a different paint effect. Older artists will be more specific about how to maneuver the ropes and brushes to create their art.

Gill Robertson's Teddy Bear Daycare kids invent another form of suspending paintbrushes on ropes...the swing set and climber!
Ropes and brushes photography 2014 Gill Robertson

More Ideas to Explore

- Look at the pictures on this page to see how brushes and ropes inspire painting in new ways!

- For a mini-version of this activity, tie one paintbrush to the center of a cord about 12 inches long. The artist can dip the brush into paint, and then pull the cord taut between his or her two hands. Explore painting on a sheet of paper with the suspended paintbrush.

Tire Roll Mural

Who can resist a motorcycle tire covered in paint, rolling down a long table on butcher paper? Check out the action of those tracks! Washing the tire with warm soapy water and scrub brushes is part of the action and a helpful way to end a great art experience.

How do we know process art encourages thinking? The answer is in the facial expressions of these young artists.

Materials

- At least two people
- Motorcycle tire (or smaller car tire)
- Long table or floor area
- Butcher paper on a roll, tape
- Tempera paints in several colors, in wide containers or bowls
- Paintbrushes, medium and large, for each color
- Tub or bucket of water for rinsing brushes, old towel or rags
- Tire washing: small buckets of warm water, soap, sponges, scrub brushes, old towels

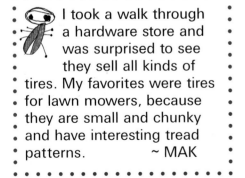

I took a walk through a hardware store and was surprised to see they sell all kinds of tires. My favorites were tires for lawn mowers, because they are small and chunky and have interesting tread patterns.   ~ MAK

Action Process

1. Pull out paper from a roll of butcher paper from one end of a long table to the other end (or floor), centering the paper in the middle of the table. Tape the paper to the table at both ends, and along the sides too.

2. Stand the tire up on the worktable at one end. Paint the tire treads. (Artists will paint other surfaces of the tire too, but it is treads that will make the tracks on the paper.) Many colors can be applied in any way.

3. At least two artists will be needed: one to roll and one to catch. One artist lines up the tire so it will roll straight (maybe), and gives it a push. It may roll all the way to the end of the table, it may fall over, it may fall off the table, or it may roll only a few inches. Exploring and experimenting is a big part of this activity. Note: Artists may discover that circle prints are made when the tire falls on its side.

4. Eventually, the artist at the other end of the table will catch the rolling tire. Now the tire can be repainted where it has landed, and sent rolling back the other way. Painting and rolling can go on as long as the pair of artists is interested.

5. Remove the paper to dry, perhaps hanging it on a wall with tape or tacks. Save the tire for another pair of artists, or store for another day.

6. Cleanup time: There will be no problem finding volunteers for cleanup. The tire can be placed on old towels on the worktable or on the floor. Scrub and wash the paint away with warm, soapy water. Dry with old towels. Hands and fingers will be clean too!

Tire photography 2014 Lakisha Reid Discovery Early Learning Center

More Ideas to Explore

- Roll a bicycle tire across butcher paper. Other tires that work well are tires from strollers and riding toys, removed and ready to paint and roll by hand.
- Ride a trike or riding toy through paint on butcher paper.
- Paint a mini-version with tiny tires and wheels.

Spin Art Bicycle Wheel

The action of squirting paint on a spinning wheel contraption made from a bicycle wheel is fun and exciting, producing fascinating art designs that kids love! Artists experiment with colors and squirting techniques to see the many ways the paint will spin.

Building the spinning wheel contraption takes a little time, but it's well worth it. Just look at the spin art and the expressive faces of the artists!

Spin photography 2014 Leigh Ann Yuen, lead teacher
Garden Gate Child Development Center
Activity Co-Creators:
Leigh Ann Yuen and Chantale Légaré

Leigh Ann Yuen comments that bicycle spin art is very messy, but also a top favorite. Her artists used paintbrushes during the spinning to change the look of paint designs. Artists also painted additional circles on the canvas after the spin art paint was dry.   ~ LAY, CL

Materials

- Bicycle wheel, old or used
- Wooden block, small, 3/4" thick
- One 4 1/2" screw to fit through the wheel as an axle
- Old worktable or tree stump
- Two 1 1/2" screws to attach the block to the worktable
- The canvas: Choose from oilcloth, canvas, heavy paper, or cardboard (cut to the size of the bicycle wheel). Note: Very large "Texas coffee filters" from Discount School Supply or restaurant supply stores make wonderful paper for this activity. You can even dampen the coffee filter with water for extra effects.
- Acrylic paint, or tempera paints in squeeze bottles (picnic ketchup and mustard bottles, or bottles from lotion or shampoo)

A block of wood and 3 screws form the central pin that holds the spinning wheel.

Action Process

1. First, the spinning screw mount must be assembled so the bicycle wheel will spin. To begin, insert a 4 1/2" screw through the center of the wood block so the point is fully through the block. Then attach this unit to an old table with the smaller screws, pointy screw sticking up and flat side down. Pre-drill holes for easier assembly. See the photograph to the left.

2. Slip the wheel over top of the 4 1/2" screw mount. It should spin. Practice spinning the wheel before adding the canvas and paint.

3. Make a hole in the center of the canvas circle. Place this over the screw and over the wheel.

4. As the wheel spins, squirt paint on the canvas, and spinning designs will rapidly form. Some artists like to add paintbrushes during the spinning to further experiment and explore design possibilities.

More Ideas to Explore

- Spin collage materials from the spinning bicycle tire to land on paper. Glue in place where items land.

- Spin collage items covered in paint, letting them spin out on paper, making designs where they land.

So much action in one spinning wheel! Artists explore (1) spinning without paint as great practice and fun, (2) squirting paint during the spin, (3) brushing paint before, during, or after spinning, and (4) adding paint after the spin art is dry. It seems there is no end to the creative possibilities of this action art activity.

Walking Paint Bags

It takes two to tango, and two to walk the long canvas carrying a pole with hanging bags of paint that trail paint responding to the artists' movements. Shaking, swinging, and swirling are a few of the wonders to behold.

Materials

- Paper or canvas, 3'x6' or longer (two 3'x6' canvases taped side-by-side make a large paint area)
- Wooden pole (dowel, broomstick, closet pole) at least 4' long
- 3 ziplock bags, gallon-size
- String, scissors
- Acrylic paint or tempera paint, 3 colors (mix with a little water so paint will flow but not be too runny)
- Plastic tarp or other floor covering

See the live video, *Action Painting*, of the artists in the photograph above creating *Walking Paint Bags* (and more):
www.youtube.com/watch?v=iO7QPjwMaMc

Paint bag photography and video, Leigh Ann Yuen 2014,
Lead Teacher Garden Gate Child Development Center
Activity Co-Creators:
Leigh Ann Yuen and Chantale Légaré

Working together can be challenging for young artists, but this activity was so phenomenal and so much fun they didn't want to stop! Observation of these artists showed they had worked out a system of being fairly careful so as not to yank the pole from each other's hands. This is a great partner activity! ~ LAY, CL

Action Process

1. Cover the floor with the plastic tarp, or choose to move the activity outdoors, where paint spatters are less of a concern. Pour about 1 cup of paint in each of the 3 ziplock bags. Add water or colors to mix in the bag. Seal the bag well. Mix paint by shaking and kneading the bag to a flowing consistency.

2. Now for the action! Two artists hold a wooden pole across one end of the long canvas, one at either end of the pole. An adult ties 3 bags of paint to the pole, fairly close together.

3. An adult snips a corner from each bag, making a drip hole so the paint can begin to flow. Right away, the artists begin walking along the length of the canvas as the paint starts to form designs on the paper or canvas.

4. Artists can move the pole in different ways over the canvas to see cause effects with their movements, like shaking, swinging, or other motions. The canvas will become filled with color and design based on the movements.

5. Two more artists, or the same artists, can take over at the end of the canvas, and walk back toward the beginning, doing more shaking of the pole and the bags with movements that cause the paint to make drips, blops, lines, and squiggles.

6. Continue until satisfied with the covering and design of the canvas. Dry well overnight as the paint designs can be very thick.

By varying paint color options, this activity lends itself to art-inspiring seasons and events. Green and yellow and pink for spring, blue-gray and white for winter, bright crimson and gold for fall, and all the other colors in between. Artists love learning new color words like scarlet, azure, indigo, *and* lime. Vermilion *is a big favorite! A list of unusual color words can be found at* **www.enchantedlearning.com/wordlist/colors/.**

More Ideas to Explore
Splatter and squirt paint with a –

- toothbrush
- water gun
- picnic squeeze bottle
- turkey baster

Blowing Melted Crayons, pages 72-73
Crayon photography Barbara Zaborowski
© *Bright Ring Publishing 2014*

3

Blowing
Exploding
Smooshing

Blown Glitter

White glue puddles are blown with a drinking straw to create fancy shapes on paper. These sticky shapes are then covered with sparkling glitter.

An artist carefully sends puffs of air to shape her glue puddle, which she then covers with glitter. Sometimes artists add confetti, punch dots, or colored sand to fill the glue.

Materials

- White glue (use full strength, or may be thinned with water in a dish)
- Spoon, optional
- Drinking straw (heavy-duty wide straws work well), one for each artist
- Drawing paper or cardstock
- Glitter in a container (multiple mixed colors of glitter can in one container)
  Optional instead of glitter: colored sand, salt, confetti, punch dots, sequins, spangles, glitter glue

*Glitter photography 2014 Gill Robertson
Teddy Bear Daycare, Souris, Manitoba, Canada*

Gill Robertson's Teddy Bear Daycare enjoys process art every day. The kids have amazing confidence and skill gained from their exposure to so many art experiences.   ~ GR

Action Process

1. Squeeze one small puddle of white glue on the paper. (If using thinned glue, spoon a puddle of glue on the paper.)

2. Aim the straw at the glue without touching the glue, and blow through the straw to force the glue into shapes on the paper. Try strong blowing and then light blowing for different effects. Note: Some artists will want to use the end of the straw to "paint" or push the glue into shapes, which also will work.

3. Before the glue dries, carefully spoon some glitter onto one of the blown glue shapes. Hint: If using different colors of glitter, do one color of glitter at a time before adding a secon color. When the shape is covered, let the glitter fall back into the container. Then change colors and add more glitter to another shape. The extra glitter can fall back into the container More than likely, all the colors will mix somewhat and will make a new container cheerfully called Multi-Color Glitter.

4. Pour more glue into puddles and blow these glue puddles into shapes.

5. Continue filling all the shapes with glitter. Note: Other materials, like colored sand, confetti, white salt, sequins, and spangles, are also artistically effective when sprinkled in the shapes.

6. The art will need to dry for about a half hour so the glue won't run, and overnight is recommended for the most portable artwork.

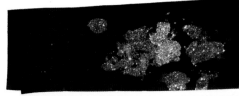

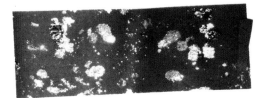

More Ideas to Explore

- Add additional sparkle to the art with glitter glue or metallic markers; snips of foil or foil wrapping paper cut in shapes adds shine.
- Add small puddles of paint and blow into shapes.
- Some artists like to glue foil shapes on the paper before blowing the glue. Over the foil, they make their glue puddles, blow the puddles into shapes, and add the glitter.

Party Blower Art

Party blowers create prints with the action of blowing and unfurling the blower into paint, letting it curl up, and then blowing it out again on paper. The feather on the end is especially fun to watch do its work. Young artists are often more focused on the festive fun of painting with a party blower than on what becomes a lovely, ethereal artwork.

If artists are offered unusual implements for painting, be prepared to see some skeptical looks from them! Imagine the looks I got when I suggested painting with party blowers. Before long the artists were totally engaged, and one boy had the grace to give me a look that said, "I'll admit it, Mrs. Zaborowski. You were right."
~ BBZ

Blowing into the party blower extends the end into paint, which then curls back as the artist takes a breath. Then repeat blowing to extend the painted blower on the paper, creating print after print. The little feather on the end is of great interest to observant artists.

Materials

- Newsprint or drawing paper
- Worktable or easel
- Tempera paints, several colors
- Paper plate
- Spoon or brush
- Party blower (personal party blower for each artist)
  Note: Sharing of party blowers is not allowed, due to health and safety precautions. Supervise children at all times.

Action Process

1. Spoon several colors of paint in small puddles on a paper plate. Three primary colors work well, but any colors are fine.

2. Give each artist a personal party blower that will not be shared. It's a good idea to write each child's name on a blower with a permanent marker.

3. Now for the action! Blow into the party blower so it extends into a paint puddle. It will then curl back up. Repeat the action, extending the blower to uncurl into the art paper, making a print. Repeat blowing toward the paper to get more than one print before adding more paint.

4. Return to the paper plate and paints. Extend the blower once again into any of the colors, and then again on the paper. Some artists like to mix the paints right on the paper plate to make new colors, and then blow the new color onto the paper.

5. Repeat the blowing and painting action until satisfied with the experience.

More Ideas to Explore

- Who can paint with two party blowers at the same time?
- Other party favors and decorations can be saved for art, such as:
  - crepe paper for making watercolor paint
  - tiny umbrellas for printing designs
  - greeting cards, ribbons, and wrapping paper for collage
  - draw with party candles and brush over the drawing with paint
- Group Art: Each artist will have a personal party blower to use throughout the project. Painting on one large piece of paper? The group may need to decide how to choose painting areas, sharing of paints, and choices of colors.

Party blower photography Barbara Zaborowski
© Bright Ring Publishing 2014

Floating Bubble Prints

Catch colorful floating bubbles on "bubble paddles," making action bubble prints by the score. This activity is setup for four artists, but you can adjust the materials to fit your needs.

Experienced preschool teacher, Zannifer Rolich, saw that some artists wanted to do both jobs, and some wanted to do only one.

   She observed a girl ask a boy how he made so many big bubbles. He showed her his system where he carefully placed the wand in the solution and began to count, "1, 2, 3 ... 8, 9, 10, 11. There! See?" Then he made some very nice large bubbles for catching. Interestingly enough, none of the two or three kids to whom he showed his system followed his instructions.   ~ ZGR

Materials

- Homemade bubble mixture for each of four pans: 1 1/2 – 2 cups Dawn dish detergent and 1/4 cup tempera paint
- Four flat pans with sides, one for each color (aluminum baking pans work well)
- Bubble wands, 4 large
- Four sticks (use extra bubble wands or any other sticks, yardsticks, dowels, rulers, flyswatters, old badminton rackets, old Ping-Pong paddles, etc.)
- White poster board or cardstock, scissors
- Duct tape and stapler
- Tempera paints, four colors (any number of colors is fine, one for each pan)

Action Process

1. First make four bubble-catching paddles. Duct-tape a sheet of cardstock to a bubble wand covering the front of the bubble-making section, and then staple a second sheet to the first, covering the back of the same area. If you don't have a wand, any stick or even a flyswatter will do.

2. Next make the bubble mixture, one color for each pan. See approximate measurements to the left. Stir each pan gently to mix paint and detergent.

3. Artists may choose to be bubble makers or bubble catchers. They can change "jobs" once the activity is underway.

4. Bubble makers dip their wands in the paint and soap, and then move about to create floating bubbles. Bubble catchers run with their paddles to catch bubbles on the cardstock. Beautiful bubble prints will remain when the bubbles pop on the paper.

5. Continue in this way until artists wish to change jobs. Everyone can have a turn to be a maker or a catcher.

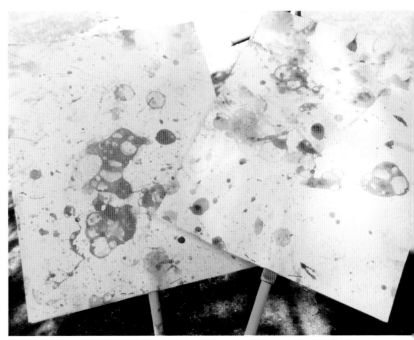

Bubble photography Zannifer Rolich 2014, University of Nevada Reno Child Care

More Ideas to Explore

- Individual artists may work with small bubble blowers or homemade bubble blowers (pipe cleaner shapes, string tied in a circle, jar lids, colanders) to make bubble prints on any kind of paper.

- Balloons make great floating prints too! Roll a balloon in liquid watercolors, and send it floating. Another artist can capture the balloon print on a paddle on a stick.

Snap Painting

Explore a snappy paint idea with glorious spatters and surprising color combinations made when rubber bands snap-paint onto paper. Wear art clothes and listen to the satisfying sound of *SNAP, SNAP, SNAP*!

Materials

- Paper
- Baking sheet with sides, or cardboard box
  (Mini-version: Use a small cardboard box and regular rubber bands)
- Large, strong rubber bands
- Paintbrushes and paints
- Sponge or damp towel for wiping paint from fingers

Rubber bands stretched over a baking sheet with sides is a snappy painting exploration for young artists. Think about varying the arrangement of bands.

Visiting a small group of first-grade boys who volunteer as my "art explorers" (they test out art activities for me) was especially inspiring the day they saw a bowl of rubber bands on the art table. I think I heard their brains make joyful snappy noises! *Ping! Zap! YAY!* The activity was a huge success, especially putting together the rubber band contraption that would produce the painting technique.

~ MAK

Action Process

1. Place a sheet of paper on the baking sheet (or in the box). This is called the frame. Wrap rubber bands around the frame. They can be close together or far apart. They can be set at one direction, or they can cross over each other. One direction is suggested for first-time snappers.

2. With a brush dipped in paint, paint the rubber bands, especially the side facing the paper. Less paint works better than too much.

3. Pull one of the rubber bands back and let it go! *Snap!* The band will snap paint onto the paper, and probably on art clothes and some surrounding areas too.

4. If you like, rotate the paper and repeat. Keep adding paint if you want richer, fuller paint splats and lines.

Snap photograph Lorie Kaehler 2014
Owner of Reading Confetti readingconfetti.com

More Ideas to Explore

• Put small blobs of paint on a paper plate or other paper. Slip the plate under clean rubber bands on a frame. Snap away! The rubber bands will splatter and snap the paint to form surprising designs and colors on the plate.

• Pull back multiple rubber bands at one time, and then release, for an especially colorful and noisy presentation.

Playdough Smoosh Surprise

If you think mixing paint colors is fun, wait until you try this color smooshing and mixing activity with playdough! All you need is plain uncolored playdough, food coloring or liquid watercolors, and a ziplock bag. Half the fun is being surprised by the action!

Materials

- Plain uncolored dough (recipes below)
- Measuring utensils, spoon, bowl
- Water, flour, salt, vegetable oil (cream of tartar powder – spice & baking aisle, optional)
- Food coloring or liquid watercolors (two or more colors)
- Ziplock bag (quart or half gallon)
- Cookie sheet, tray, or towel
- Finger or toothpick

Child-care art teacher Zannifer Rolich observed kids exploring this color activity with dough. Artists smooshed dough inside a bag but were much more interested in mixing the dough by hand outside the bag, which she encouraged. One artist made a roll of dough as tall as he is – exactly! (See photo, p. 67.)
~ ZR, MAK

White Clay Dough
In a saucepan, mix 1/2 cup cornstarch, 1 cup salt, and 1 cup boiling water. Boil and stir until the mixture is like a soft ball of dough. Then knead on wax paper. A wet cloth will keep the clay-dough moist if needed.

Easy Playdough
Mix 2 1/2 cups flour, 1/2 cup salt, 1 1/2 T. cream of tartar (in baking and spice aisle, for freshness but NOT required), and 1/4 cup vegetable oil. Mix in 2 cups boiling water. Knead when cool. Store in sealed plastic bag.

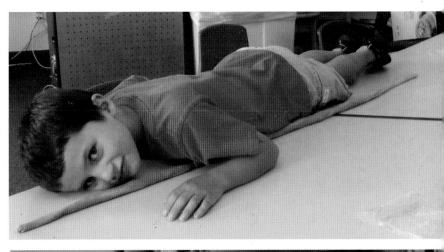

Action Process

1. Make up a batch of dough, but do not add color. Kids can help an adult with measuring. Dough recipes on page 66.

2. Pinch off some dough and make some balls about 2" in diameter, or a bit larger. Kids can easily help. Place the balls on a cookie sheet, tray, or towel.

3. This step is the "surprise element," so decide if kids will be involved. Poke a little hole halfway into each ball with a finger, toothpick, or other utensil. Place a very small drop of one color in each ball. Then seal over the hole without letting the color leak out.

4. Place two balls that are complementary in color in a ziplock bag. For example, colors when mixed together make a new color: yellow and blue, pink and yellow, blue and red, and so on. Hint: You can place more than two balls in one bag, but for beginners, two is good. Older kids will like having more balls of dough to work with.

5. Now for the smooshing action surprise! Give the artist a bag with surprise dough balls inside. Suggest the artist try smooshing the balls inside the bag without opening the bag. They can smoosh, press, pat, squeeze, or any other technique they like. Very soon, they will see the plain dough changing color, and then mixing with the other color or colors! The dough becomes an all-new color! Note: Most artists want to open the bag and smoosh by hand, which is also a good activity.

6. To help artists understand how this surprise came about, invite them to help make more colorful balls for the next round of smooshing. Knowing the secret can make the action of smooshing more artistically meaningful.

Dough photography Zannifer Rolich, University of Nevada Reno Child Care, 2014

Sparkle Spray Foam

Hand sprayers deliver the vinegar and baking soda action that will create fizzing, foaming, sparkling colors. Measurements are all approximate, so be confident when experimenting.

Materials

- Baking pan with sides
- Baking soda
- Food coloring or liquid watercolors
- White vinegar in small paper cups, one for each color
- Hand-spray bottles or misting bottles, one for each color
- Liquid dish soap
- Glitter
- Spoons or sticks for stirring
- Toy hammer or small wood block for crushing baking soda lumps, optional (see photo to the right)

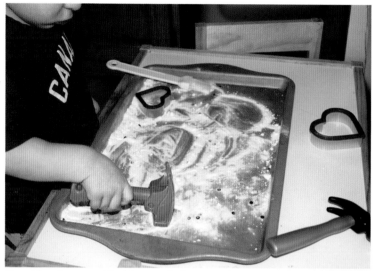

Crushing lumps of baking soda is an active way to begin.

While working with kids doing sparkle spray foam, one first-grade artist looked up from the fizzing paint and said, "Mrs. Kohl, you have the best job in the world!"   ~ MAK

Glitter adds color, sparkle, and intrigue.

Action Process

1. Spread baking soda on the bottom of a baking pan with sides. Note: Some artists sprinkle glitter over the baking soda at this point, while others wait until the foam is ready. Baking soda can be lumpy, and what better way to increase the art action than by crushing the lumps with a toy hammer, mallet, or small block of wood?

2. Pour a little vinegar in each small paper cup. Add a little food coloring or liquid watercolors to each cup to color the vinegar. Add a little squirt of liquid dish soap to each cup to increase the bubbling and foaming action. Stir gently.

3. Next, pour the vinegar mixture into individual child-sized spray or misting bottles, one bottle for each color. If you only want one color, then one spray bottle will do.

4. Spray the vinegar mixture on the baking soda, changing colors whenever you like. The foaming and fizzing will begin right away! Sprinkle glitter into the foam to add sparkle at any time.

5. Want more action? When the foaming settles down, add more baking soda to the pan, and repeat the mixing and spraying steps all over again.

Spray photography Susan Lively 2014
Owner, One Time Through, onetimethrough.com

Foam color pan photography
Amanda Rueter 2014
Writer/founder, dirtandboogers.com

Colors are explored with vinegar and baking soda.

More Ideas to Explore

- Individual foam bowl: Spoon baking soda into a bowl. Drip plain or colored vinegar on the baking soda to see the bowl fill with fizzy foam.
- Eyedropper foam: Fill small bowls with vinegar and coloring. Spread baking soda in a pan with sides. Drip and drop colored vinegar on the baking soda.

Clear Color Squish

Get into the action of squishing colorful pieces of non-hardening modeling clay between two clear acrylic frames or panels of Plexiglas to see the flattening and mixing of colors.

Artists often like to work on paper before trying out the clear plastic technique.

Materials

- Non-hardening modeling clay, or play clay (A few suggested brands: Crayola Modeling Clay, Plastilina by Jovi, Claytoon Modeling Clay, EZ Shape Modeling Clay, Toysmith Rainbow Clay)
- Two pieces of clear acrylic plastic or Plexiglas, about 8"x10" or smaller. Note: The clear plastic will get smeared and cloudy after a while, so when ready, wash with soapy hot water to remove residue.

Safety tip: Low-quality overly thin acrylic frames could break during the pressing step, so be cautious. Thick, quality acrylic frames or Plexiglas are best.

At a community art fair in Port Townsend, Washington, a group of teenagers discovered our squishing play clay art station and stayed for three hours creating abstracts, dragonflies, flowers, and more. Other kids came and went, but the teens stayed on for the entire afternoon.

~ MAK

Action Process

1. Soften the play clay by hand. Make a ball of each color.

2. Pull a small pinch from one of the colors, and stick it on one of the clear plastic panels. The clay should not be overly thick – a quarter inch is thick enough. Add more small balls and pieces of clay randomly or create a scene or picture. All efforts are acceptable.

3. Take the second sheet of clear plastic and place it over the first, lining up the edges slightly.

4. Now for the action! Leaving the clay panel flat on the table, press the top panel down, with strong, even pressure, using both hands to cover the top piece. Press and press downward to flatten the clay balls. The clay will squish and flatten slowly and surely.

5. For more action, rock the plastic with both hands pressing down, just a little, to achieve even more flattening and mixing of the balls of play clay. Try a twisting motion to further spread color in a new way.

6. When the squishing is complete, the art is complete as well.
   Note: The play clay will not harden, so it may be displayed for a very long time. It's best to let the artists know in advance that this is a temporary art activity, that the sheets will be pulled apart at some point, and that the clay will be peeled away and most likely used again. Some art is like that!

Colors glow with light when placed near a window.

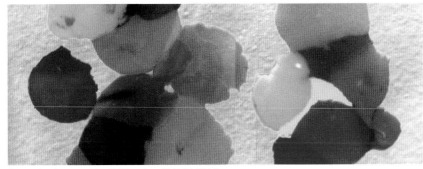

Smoosh photography © MaryAnn F. Kohl 2014

More Ideas to Explore

- The same squishing activity can be done with tempera paints. Paint on one plastic panel and then press the second panel down over the paint.
- Squish pieces of play clay between two sheets of clear plastic wrap or in a plastic bag. Rolling pin, anyone?

Blowing Melting Crayons

Create beautiful art with broken crayon stubs and a blow-dryer. Consider this an introduction to many more art activities with melted crayons, known professionally in the art world as encaustic painting.

Materials

- Paper, any kind
- Box, low-sided, big enough to hold the paper
- Crayons without paper covers (soak in water overnight and paper will fall off easily)
- Wooden ruler
- Blow-dryer (assign one to art supplies for future activities)

Kids will see all sorts of images in the splatters and shapes made by melting crayons. They may need encouragement to first "see," but once they get going, it will be like looking at fluffy clouds and imagining the shapes of elephants, cats, bunnies, wild horses, and other imaginings.   ~ BBZ

A ruler helps steady the crayon pieces so they won't blow away.

Action ART © 2015 Bright Ring Publishing

Action Process

1. Place the paper in the box. Choose a crayon to melt and place it on the paper.

2. An adult or other child can hold the crayon in place with the ruler.

3. Turn on the blow-dryer and hold its nozzle close to the crayon. It may take a few minutes for the crayon to warm up and begin to melt. Be patient. Note: It can be hard for the artist to see what is happening because the blow-dryer blocks the view. Watch for the crayon to become super-shiny, or for bits of the crayon to start spraying away. Once the crayon is melting, it will be easy to see the crayon spray spreading out.

4. Decide when to change to another crayon color, and when melted artwork is complete.
   Hint: Some artists lose interest quickly and others will want to go on forever, layering the melted crayon over other melted crayons.

5. The art will dry quickly. Depending on the paper used, the wax may make the paper transparent.

Encaustic Painting

1. Put crayons of a similar color in paper cups and melt them on a warming tray. (Look for cups with flat bottoms.)

2. Leave the cups on the warming tray and dip brushes or Q-tips (cotton buds) in the melted wax. Then paint on paper.
   Hint: The artist will need to work quickly because the wax will harden quickly. Wax can be softened again with a blow-dryer or placed back on the warming tray.

Melted crayon photography Barbara Zaborowski
© Bright Ring Publishing 2014

More Ideas to Explore

Glue several crayons on a piece of paper. They can be in specific designs or glued randomly. When the glue is completely dry, melt the crayons with the blow-dryer. Move the blow-dryer around to send melted wax in all directions.

Balloon Paint Bursts

Who doesn't love popping balloons with all the excitement and anticipation of the explosion and the noise? Get ready for explosions of laughter and expressions of amazement with paint-filled balloons that burst on paper, making some truly stunning art. Loud noise is to be expected, so plan accordingly.

Before (above) and after (below).

Balloon photography Crystal Underwood 2014 Parent/blog owner, growingajeweledrose.com

Adventurous mom Crystal Underwood and her two young daughters chose to experiment outdoors with action-packed balloon bursts. Festooned in art clothes and sunglasses, a family memory to last a lifetime was created (along with some pretty cool art).
~ CU

Materials

- Medium-size paper, like easel newsprint or 9"x12" construction paper
- Water balloons (any small–medium balloons) SUPERVISE BROKEN BALLOON PIECES CAREFULLY
- Tempera paints, multiple colors
- Several funnels, one per color makes filling go faster
- Old towel/paper towels for drying and wiping
- Cardboard box with low sides (cutting down a larger box works great), or large paper on the ground
- Popper Tools: Bamboo skewers (More suggested tools, as appropriate for age: open paper clips, toothpicks, pencils SUPERVISE TOOLS AND POPPING AT ALL TIMES
- Balloon pump, optional

Balloons make superb circle prints when dipped in paint and pressed on paper. Read page 75 for more ideas.

Action Process

1. To fill the small water balloons: Stretch open the opening, insert a small funnel, and pour in a little paint (a few tablespoons is plenty). Note: Liquid watercolors are easy to pour, but tempera paint gives a better, absolutely fantastic effect.

2. Before tying off the balloon, an adult will blow up the balloon the usual way – blowing into the opening. (A balloon pump will keep paint off the adult's lips, but really, a pump isn't necessary and the blowing and tying is quite easy. Damp paper towels can wipe the small bit of paint away.) Tie off each balloon as it is filled.

3. Shake the balloon a little to spread out the paint, which is not necessary, but is fun to do.

4. Place a sheet of paper in the bottom of the low-sided box or on paper on the ground. Place a few paint-filled balloons on the paper.

5. Ready for the action? The artist pokes a balloon with the skewer, until it … bursts! Paint explosion! Poke and explode all the balloons and see the patterns of paint and how colors mix. (Note: Some artists leave the balloon pieces in the paint to dry as part of the art, and others pick out and remove the pieces. Supervise pieces carefully.)

6. Several hands will be needed to remove the sheet of paper to a drying area if it is very heavy with wet paint. Replace with a fresh sheet of paper, and continue exploding paint balloons.

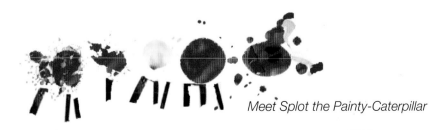

Meet Splot the Painty-Caterpillar

Paint spots can be creatively incorporated into a drawing or other artwork. The funny faces above show paint splot details.

The caterpillar collage, lower left, shows paint splot segments cut-and-pasted on paper, with added cut-and-paste legs.

More Ideas to Explore

- Fill balloons with a matching paint color, or balloons can be filled at random for a surprise color effect.
- See illustration above: Make one paint explosion on colored paper. When dry, cut out the shape. Glue it on a contrasting color paper. Some artists turn paint splots into monsters, aliens, or other imaginary creatures. Add yarn scraps, wiggly eyes, or collage materials.
- Tie a balloon to a yardstick and make prints on paper.

Zippy Paint Explosion

Vinegar and powdered tempera paint, or crushed chalk, provide the reaction that will explode a ziplock plastic sandwich bag, causing a very surprising visual paint extravaganza!

Materials

- Ziplock plastic bag, sandwich size
- 1/3 cup vinegar
- 2 tablespoons powdered tempera paint or crushed chalk
- Large craft or butcher paper, or poster board
- Outdoor area, on the ground

Do you know the Secret of the Paint Explosions?

Chalk and powdered tempera paint have limestone in them. The limestone and vinegar form carbon dioxide, and this gas is what pops the bag, a reaction known as a base and acid reaction. Note: If you don't have tempera or colored chalk, you can use baking soda and food coloring instead.

Paint explosion photography Crystal Underwood 2014, Parent/blog owner, growingajeweledrose.com

Action Process

1. Place the large paper on the ground – outdoors recommended.

2. Add 1/3 cup vinegar to a ziplock plastic bag. Then add 2 tablespoons of powdered tempera paint or crushed chalk. Quickly seal the bag.
   Important: Don't squeeze the air out or the explosion won't work. Even a tiny hole will stop the fun, so seal the bag completely.

3. Set the bag on the paper and watch it puff up and expand with gas. The bag will expand until ... it ... POPS! Fizzing paint explodes on the paper! What excitement, and so pretty!

4. Make up more bags with different colors and place them all on the paper. They should expand and pop at about the same time. Sometimes, if one doesn't explode, you have to smack it or pop it with a finger like the little girl in the photos to the right. (In that case, why not fingerpaint a bit?)

Popping the expanded bag of chalk and vinegar is an action just bursting with anticipation!

Paint explosion photography above, Amanda Sipple 2014, messyhandslessonplans.com

More Ideas to Explore

- Instead of paper, let the bags explode on the sidewalk, playground, or driveway. Color can be hosed away, or let the rain do the work.
- Try mixing two primary colors in a bag and watch the colors mix as the bag expands. Then POW!

Plunger Push Print, pages 82-83
Photography Deanna Pecaski McLennan 2014
Ontario Kindergarten teacher,
and mom of three

4

Toys
Tools
Utensils

Beat & Whisk Paint

Have you ever scrambled eggs with a manual eggbeater or whisk? Then you are ready to try the same action with paint – an energetic exploration using kitchen cooking utensils.

Asia Citro's daughter is an experienced artist due to her mom's at-home learning experiences with activities from her blog, FUNATHOMEWITHKIDS.COM. Miss S. especially loved using an electric mixer for painting and was very successful in managing the paint, the mixer, and the art. Remember that process art experiences help build confident, capable people.
~ AC, MAK

Above, and below left: A variety of ages in this family allows for everyone to create together, each at individual paces and ability levels.

Materials

- Eggbeater, handheld manual (or plastic toy eggbeater)
- Kitchen whisk, manual
- Tempera paints in wide-mouthed containers, one for each color
- Large paper
- Rinse water in a tub or bucket
- Old towels or rags
- Damp sponges

Below: This adventurous artist prefers the action of an electric mixer, which she handles beautifully. Her mom, Asia Citro (funathomewithkids), is watching closely.

knitinmywomb.blogspot.com 2014   Amanda Sipple 2014   Asia Citro 2014   Asia Citro 2014

Action Process One

Eggbeater

1. Set out paint in containers with wide enough openings to accommodate the eggbeater rotors. Dip the eggbeater in one color of paint. Let some extra paint drip back into the cup.

2. Rest the eggbeater rotors on the paper, hold in place, and start cranking by hand to spin the rotors and cause the paint to splatter out onto the paper. Move the eggbeater to a new spot and keep cranking.

3. When changing colors, dip the eggbeater into the clear water and give it some vigorous cranks to rinse off paint. Dry the rotors briefly with a rag or old towel. Then try another color. Dip the eggbeater in paint and repeat the process and action.

4. Experiment with holding the eggbeater above the paper, not touching. Sponges will come in handy for catching spatters.

Action Process Two

Whisk

1. Proceed as with the eggbeater, dipping the whisk basket in paint. Hold the whisk with the basket touching the paper. Roll the handle between hands like rolling a clay snake to spin the whisk and cause the paint to fly off onto the paper. Note: Most artists simply like to fling the paint, and this is perfectly acceptable as a painting method.

2. Rinse the whisk if needed, and blot to dry. Continue to dip in one or more paint colors, and repeat motions (or experiment with new ways to whisk the paint onto the paper). For example, try holding the whisk above the paper, not touching, and see the results.
Hint: Damp sponges come in handy for catching spatters.

The action of a manual eggbeater creates intriguing paint patterns and shapes as artists develop new skills.
Photography, Asia Citro 2014

More Ideas to Explore

- Search the kitchen and find other utensils that might be fun for paint exploration. Some ideas are: spatula, fork, tongs, spreader, and grater.

- If you decide to try an electric mixer, use caution, supervise closely, and one child at a time only. Begin with the lowest speed before progressing to higher speeds.

Plunger Push Print

Making prints with plungers involves muscle and big action movement. Dipping a plunger in paint and pressing it on paper produces numerous circle prints. One plunger for each color of paint keeps colors bright.

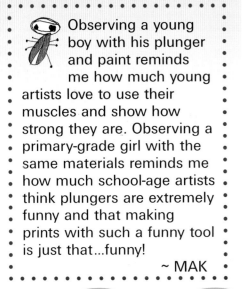

Observing a young boy with his plunger and paint reminds me how much young artists love to use their muscles and show how strong they are. Observing a primary-grade girl with the same materials reminds me how much school-age artists think plungers are extremely funny and that making prints with such a funny tool is just that...funny!

~ MAK

Young artists use big muscle action to make plunger push prints.

Materials

- Paper, any kind (big is best)
- Floor protection (shower curtain, tarp, trash bags, newspaper)
- Tempera paints, variety of colors
- Grocery trays or flat pans for paint
- Pieces of foam or sponge cut to the size of the paint trays, optional (moisten sponge with water and squeeze out excess, which helps cut down globbing of paint)
- Toilet plungers, ideally one for each color of paint (available at dollar stores, often in two different sizes)

Plunger photography Deanna Pecaski McLennan 2014 Ontario Kindergarten Teacher/Full Day Kindergarten Mom to three amazing children

A pie pan is the perfect size for plunger and paint.

Action Process

1. Set up the floor area with protection and paper.

2. Place damp sponges in the grocery trays to work as a printing pad and to help control paint "globbing."

3. Pour paint on the sponges, each sponge with a different color. No sponges? Pour paint directly on the tray.

4. Set a plunger on each tray of paint directly on the paint or sponge pad.

5. Ready for the big muscle action? Press the plunger into the paint, and then press on the paper to make prints. Note: Most artists will use a lot of muscle to do this, which is why this activity works best on the floor.

6. Repeat with as many colors as desired.
   Hint: If only one plunger is being used, it can be rinsed and/or wiped quickly between colors.
   Hint: Allowing colors to mix on the plunger will produce mixed-color prints and unique effects, a favorite of young artists.

More Ideas to Explore

- Dip half the plunger rim in one color and the other half in a second color. Mix colors on one pad for multi-colors.
- Paint the plunger rim with a brush rather than dipping in paint. This is a slower process for very young artists.
- Plunger Ringers: Make plunger ringers with black paint or any other dark color. Then brush paint in the circle shapes with additional paint colors. Where circles prints overlap (if they do), change interior paint colors.

Sanded Paint Block

Sandpaper and vigorous arm actions transform a brightly painted block of wood into a subtle revision of the original. Most artists can't seem to get enough of sanding wood, so plan extra time!

Four-year-old Jacob (not pictured) is an energetic artist when wood or tools are involved – on cloud nine and ready to roll. On Monday, he carefully painted his block of wood, and let it dry overnight. Tuesday morning, he was wearing work goggles, a carpenter apron, and held sheets of sandpaper squares in both hands. Jacob sanded his block until smooth, with very little color left. He was extremely pleased with his work.   ~ MAK

The action of sanding painted wood captures the imagination and focus of artists of all ages.

Materials

- Sandpaper
- Block (or short section of wooden board), unfinished and clean
- Tempera paints or liquid watercolors in containers or cups
- Paintbrushes, any kind
- Work goggles are a good idea (and inspiring!)
- Damp rag, optional

Liquid watercolors were used to paint the wood block.

Action Process

1. Place the clean block of wood on the workspace with paints and brushes nearby.

2. Turn the block of wood over and over to look at all its surfaces.

3. With tempera paints or liquid watercolors, brush color onto the block of wood in any design or picture. Cover edges as well as flat areas.

4. Dry until color does not come off on hands. Overnight is a good idea, but an hour should be long enough.

5. Put on work goggles. Look at the painted wood block. Think about which parts or colors to remove by sanding. Begin sanding with vigorous arm movements and focused energy. Sand to remove paint and design in chosen areas, including edges of the block. Sometimes the sandpaper will need to be folded or turned to gain more use of the rough sand. (Note: Some children will remove all paint and all color.)

6. When satisfied with the results of sanding, artists may take a damp rag and gently brush away sawdust that is clinging to the block. Some artists like to use a damp rag to wipe away even more paint!

Block photos Barbara Zaborowski
© Bright Ring Publishing 2014

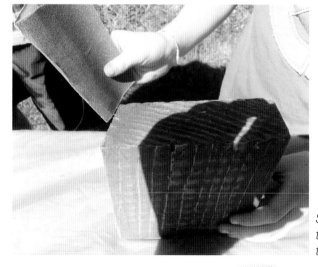

Sanding the block removes the paint color, showing off the smoothed wood grain.

More Ideas to Explore

- Substitute a square of cardboard or a cardboard box for wood.
- Markers instead of paint work great! Designs and colors may be sanded to fade or to completely disappear.
- Crayons may be used but removal fills sandpaper with wax. Light crayon marks are easiest to sand.

Toy Top Flashy Spin

Inexpensive toy tops of the plastic party favor variety (or any tops purchased or homemade) are dipped in paint and then spun on paper to create spatters and swirls. Add a little glitter here and there to increase the flashy gleam and shine.

Materials

- Toy tops, inexpensive plastic party favor variety (usually come in a bag of six small tops). Note: Some people make their own tops with Tinkertoys or by other means.
- Large box lid with sides to hold paper, and paper to fit in box
- Tempera paint (poster paint) or liquid watercolors in cups or containers about 1″ deep with paint
- Glitter glue in squeeze bottles or glitter and glue (metallic colors are a favorite)
- Damp sponge on table for wiping fingers
- Tub of water, and towel or rags for rinsing

*Tinkertoy spinning tops photography Gill Robertson 2014
Teddy Bear Daycare, Souris, Manitoba, Canada*

Gill Robertson of Teddy Bear Daycare says she searched everywhere for a toy top, including party supply departments and thrift stores where she always finds whatever she needs for art. She decided to make her own top with a Tinkertoy, marble, and glue. (See photos.)   ~ GR

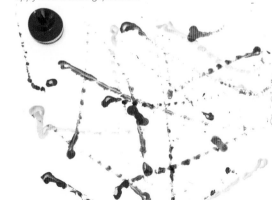

*Photo below: Betsy Kortenkamp 2014
tippytoecrafts.blogspot.com*

Action Process

1. Before making the spinning top painting, practice spinning tops on the floor or table. Use the pincer hold with pointer and thumb. Twist the top a bit, and off it zooms! Practice as long as artists are interested, often enough for one day.

2. When ready, fill cups with paint. The cup must be wide enough to dip a toy top inside. Arrange paint cups next to large box lid. Place paper in the large box lid.

3. To start the action, dip a top about halfway into a cup of paint. Then without waiting, spin the top in the box lid on the paper. The top will spin about, flinging paint in small bursts and spatters of color, often bumping into the walls.

4. Continue dipping and spinning with more colors. Rinsing and drying the top now and then helps keep the colors bright.

5. When satisfied, remove the paper to another work area. Add squeezes and dots of glitter glue here and there. Then allow the artwork to dry completely.

6. Meanwhile, add a clean sheet of paper to the box lid for another painting or another artist. Repeat steps.

These tops are homemade with Tinkertoys! They spin beautifully through puddles of paint, or when dipped in paint and then spun on paper.

Construct an easy spinning top with a Tinkertoy, a peg, and a marble.

More Ideas to Explore

- Cover an entire worktable with wide craft or butcher paper, and tape corners to hold. A small group can spin several tops at once as an active group painting. Tops will crash into each other, so don't be surprised!

- Turn the lights low, and shine a flashlight on the glittery paintings for an *oooo-ahhh* art moment. Sunlight makes them shine.

Windup Toy Tracks

Small windup toys hop, jump, and dance their way across paper creating art designs and tracks with two mechanical art explorations kids will love.

Windup toys of all kinds are ready for action!

Artists will enjoy all the windup toys you may have. My kids especially love the small plastic monkey that does backflips! When looking for toys, keep an eye out for those with different kinds of feet and walkers that will produce a variety of tracks. Bring out this activity when you've collected four or five windup toys. Ask friends or families to donate ones they may have on hand.   ~ BBZ

The artist helps a windup monkey make wiggly tracks.

Materials

- Windup toys with various abilities (walking, pecking, rocking, spinning, etc.)
- Flat work area: table, floor, or pan with sides
- Paper
- Liquid watercolors or other paint
- Tape
- Cotton balls
- Thread

Hint: A windup toy with a pecking action, like a chicken or duck, will work especially well for dots. Toys that walk in one direction make great lines with varying widths. Every toy offers a different design discovery.

Action Process One

Windup Tracks

1. Place the sheet of paper on the table or on a baking pan with sides. (The sides will help keep the windup toy from wandering too far.)

2. Place drops of liquid watercolors (or other paint) on the paper here and there in any way.

3. Wind up a toy, place it on the paper, and let it walk through the paint, making tracks as it goes. Pick up the toy and replace it as often as you like. Add more paint as needed. See the designs that a windup toy can make walking or moving through paint in different ways.

Action Process Two
Windup Tug Along

1. Place a clean sheet of paper on the baking pan or table as before.

2. Tie a 6"-10" length of sewing thread to the windup toy. Tie the other end to a fluffy cotton ball. Dip the cotton ball into a shallow cup of liquid watercolors thinned with water. Do not squeeze out the extra.

3. Wind the toy. Place the toy with its thread and cotton ball on the paper and let it pull the cotton ball across the paper, making marks and designs as it moves.

4. Change colors, cotton balls, positions, or types of windups at any time.
   Note: If you prefer, skip the cotton ball, and dip the yarn or thread in paint. Place the windup toy on the paper, and see it pull the strand across the paper. Experimenting with materials allows for new ideas and action.

Mr. Monkey, a great favorite windup toy of young artists, wiggle-walks in paint, and then stops to see his tracks.

Teeth Choppers waddle across the paper.

Windup toy photography Barbara Zaborowski © Bright Ring Publishing 2014

More Ideas to Explore

- Tape a marker or Q-tip to a windup toy so the tip touches the paper. If using a Q-tip, first dip one end in liquid watercolors. (The marker has its own color.) Wind the toy, place it on the paper, and let it drag or tap the paint-dipped Q-tip or marker across the paper.

Electric Toothbrush Designs

Painting with an electric toothbrush is not only an artistic experience, but it is sensory as well. Young artists particularly enjoy holding a buzzing, shaking, humming toothbrush. In fact, nearly every child – and some adults too! – count electric toothbrush art as an all-time favorite action art experience.

Karyn (TEACHBESIDEME.COM) was surprised her young artists enjoyed painting with electric toothbrushes so much they wanted to put the brushes back by the bathroom sink to use again! Let your kids know art toothbrushes will remain in the art area, and can be used again and again – *for art*!   ~ KT

Toothbrush photography page 90, Karyn Tripp, teachbesideme.com

Materials

- Electric toothbrushes (inexpensive in dollar stores), charged and ready
- Tempera paints or liquid watercolors
- Shallow containers or flat pans
- Paper, any kind
- Damp sponges for wiping hands

Action Process

1. Charge up one electric toothbrush for each paint color. If you only have one, one is enough to use with multiple colors. Place the toothbrush on the workspace, turned off to begin.

2. Pour paints into containers, one container for each color. A shallow container about 1″-2″ deep works well.

3. Dip the toothbrush in one color of paint. Turn on the toothbrush. Paint on the paper with the vibrating bristles.

4. Change colors and brushes as you wish.

Note: This is a good project for a small group to work on together.

Hint: Damp sponges work well for quick wipes of paint-covered hands.

Toothbrush photography page 91, Suja Balaji, blogmemom.com

A toothbrush vibrating unassisted on the paper makes surprise designs.

More Ideas to Explore

- Place the toothbrush on its side on the paper and watch it paint on its own as it moves and shakes paint on the paper.
- Stand the toothbrush up on the butt end of its handle, turn it on, and see if it will stand and vibrate while shaking paint on the paper.
- Place several "on" toothbrushes on the paper all at once and see what designs emerge.

Chalk Rake

Draw, design, and write big-and-beautiful on outdoor blacktop or sidewalks using a homemade chalk rake. Jumbo chalk, some duct tape, and a rake: that's all you need!

Materials

- Garden rake
- Jumbo chalk
- Duct tape or masking tape
- Outdoor area, such as a sidewalk, playground, driveway, patio

Note: Chalk sticks often break during energetic raking. Replace or carry on without. The broken pieces can be used for drawing by hand when the artist tires of using the rake.

Large chalk sticks are taped between the tines of a garden rake, allowing for active raking and designing by this young artist. A damp sidewalk will produce even brighter colors than a dry one. Chalk is a perfect "after rain" art activity. No rain? Spray the chalk drawings with water in handheld misting bottles.

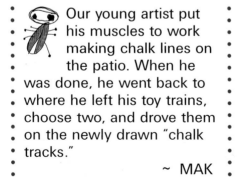

Our young artist put his muscles to work making chalk lines on the patio. When he was done, he went back to where he left his toy trains, choose two, and drove them on the newly drawn "chalk tracks."

~ MAK

Action Process

1. Adult steps 1 and 2: Press a stick of jumbo colored chalk between the teeth of the garden rake. Skip a space between teeth, and add another stick of chalk. Use as many sticks as the rake will hold. The drawing ends should be at the same length as much as possible.

2. Next secure the sticks of chalk in place with duct tape, wrapping around the rake and chalk sticks several times. The teeth of the rake and the tape will securely hold the chalk.

3. The artist simply "rakes" the blacktop or sidewalk, finding ways to make lines, designs, and drawings.

4. Some artists will make long, winding rainbow trails; others will write their names or draw shapes. The process of discovery will lead the artist to explore how chalk behaves on blacktop or a sidewalk.

Chalk rake photography © MaryAnn F. Kohl 2014

More Ideas to Explore

- Two artists can play Follow the Leader, with one child drawing a trail to follow, and the other following. They can trade places and repeat the drawing game!
- Explore drawing on wet blacktop or sidewalk surfaces. Spray lightly with a hose, or go outside when the rain stops. The water will brighten the chalk lines considerably.

R/C Car Race Art

Rev up making tracks with radio control cars (remote control cars) driving through paint. Some artists like to paint the wheels and then let 'em roll!

Materials

- Outdoor area
  (No outdoor area? Use a cardboard box with sides cut about 2"-3" high.)
- BIG paper (or paper to fit in the box)
- Tempera paints in cups or squeeze bottles with paintbrushes and/or spoons
- R/C electric cars with controllers

Note: R/C cars found at the dollar store have a short wire attached from the controller to the car and work as well as wireless R/C cars.

The kids were so excited about playing with the cars that we gave them a good long time to practice maneuvering them with confidence before adding paint. Good thing we did! Their approach to the art was skillful and creative.
~ MAK

R/C car photos, Barbara Zaborowski © Bright Ring Publishing 2014

Car photos above: April Barlett 2014, Elementary art teacher, Virginia

Action Process

1. Spread out paper on the ground outdoors, or in the box with sides indoors.

2. Pour some small puddles of paint on the paper. A spoon or paintbrush has good control for dripping or dropping. Some artists prefer to paint the wheels of the car while others prefer driving through puddles of color.

3. Place an R/C car on the paper, turn on the control, and drive the car through the paint. The outdoor art activity needs big paper, several sheets taped together if possible, for fast and colorful tracks and designs. If using the cardboard box, the car will go around and around, bumping into the sides of the box, sometimes turning over, and making colorful tracks.

4. Refresh paper as needed, and add more paint at any time during the activity.

Allow for play-practice with the cars before the art activity.

R/C cars are raced through puddles of paint on large paper – action-packed art!

More Ideas to Explore

- Place more than one car in the car-racing and painting box at a time.
- Substitute pull-back cars – toy cars that go forward after being "wound" by pulling them back and letting them go on their own.
- Drive regular toy cars by hand in paint and then on paper to make tracks.

Tricycle Circles

Use those leg muscles to pedal a trike through paint, creating colorful tracks and a continuous mixing of colors.

Materials

- Tempera paints in squeeze bottles
- Large paper (craft paper, butcher paper, old posters), taped together for a wide riding area
- Tricycle or bicycle (other wheeled toys also welcome)
- Pan of soapy water, rags, sponges, and other cleanup supplies

Trike photography Naomi Yalkowsky Foster 2014, Preschool teacher, Tucson Jewish Community Center

Paper ready? Check. Sunny day? Check. Paint ready? Check. Trike ready? Check. Kids ready? YES!

One little girl in particular doesn't usually like to get messy, but here she is in her ballet costume (ballet is right after school, so she is prepared), riding through paint (THIRD PHOTO DOWN ON LEFT).   ~ NYF

Action Process

1. Spread out the paper. Working outdoors is recommended but indoors works well too. Squirt blobs and puddles of paint here and there on the paper.

2. The artist rides through the paint on the paper, making tracks with the trike or bike.

3. In the activity pictured to the left, numerous children took turns riding through paint, sharing the original painting, increasing the tracks, and color mixing throughout the morning.

4. When done, most artists will be enthused about scrubbing and drying – and polishing – the riding toy.

*Bike photography Suzanne Axelsson 2014,
Preschool teacher, Filosofiska, Sweden
interactionimagination.blogspot.se*

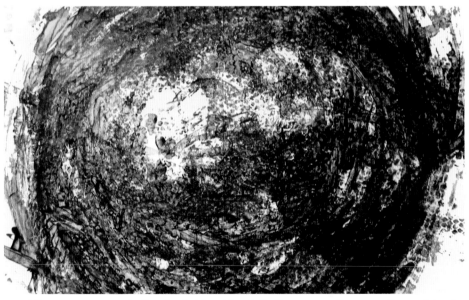

After everyone rode the "paint tracking trike" as many times as they wished, the final result left tracks that told the story of their art process.

More Ideas to Explore

Explore other riding and wheeled toys, such as:

- Skateboards, skates, bikes
- Radio-controlled cars
- Pull-back cars
- Toy trains, trucks, toy cars of all sizes
- Baby walker

Drill Painting

Painting with an electric drill? Really? Yes! Insert a paintbrush where the drill bit usually goes, tighten, and paint a twirly, whirly painting.

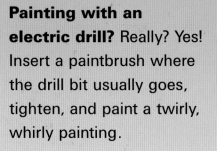 Sibling Art: When the brother first began to paint with the drill, the brush came apart in pieces and we were all laughing and enjoying the surprise "bad start." A new paintbrush was inserted and he went on to work diligently as he discovered how to create beautiful soft edges with the brush "drilling" on its side.

His younger sister used both hands to hold the heavy drill at an angle on the easel. She was intent on her unique art and was not at all deterred by the weight of the drill.

Both kids say they LOVE this activity!   ~ MAK

Materials

- Electric drill, cordless, battery charged
- Paint easel
- Strong paper, poster board, or cardstock (not newsprint)
- Tempera paints, many colors
- Easel cups or containers
- Duct tape

Kids in a local kindergarten voted drill painting as #1 of their ten favorite action art activities!

Drill photography B. Zaborowski © Bright Ring Publishing 2014

Red drill photo Ann Harquail 2014, Owner, mynearestanddearest.com

Action Process

1. Charge up a cordless electric drill, the kind that has a battery pack, which allows the artist freedom to hold the drill comfortably and safely.

2. Fill each paint cup about 1" deep with tempera paint, one color per cup. Enjoy using many colors. (Idea: Consider colors to match a specific season or holiday.) Place a loop of duct tape on the bottom of each cup to help hold the cup steady during the activity.

3. Clip paper to the easel. Strong paper that won't tear easily works best. (Idea: Consider a sheet of Plexiglas to paint on rather than paper.)

4. Insert a paintbrush in the drill bit and tighten. Only one brush will be used for all the colors. Practice first: Turn the drill off and on, go fast and go slow, and find a comfortable hold.

5. Ready for drill action? With the drill turned off, dip the brush into a cup of paint, and then point the brush close to or touching the paper. Now squeeze the trigger to start the drill. Paint with the spinning brush. The brush will try to whirl across the paper, and that is part of the design and excitement. Controlling the brush and paint will happen little by little with experience. More than one sheet of paper will be needed as skills improve.

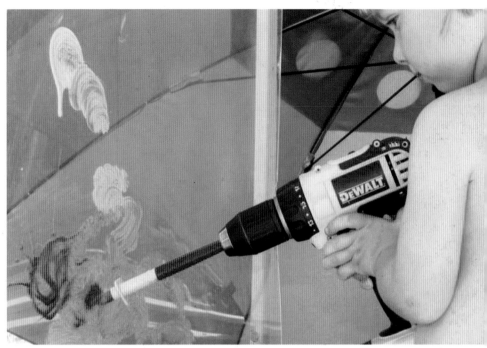

Drill painting on Plexiglas is a painting option where paper is not needed. Very washable!
Plexiglas photography Playathomemomllc.com 2014

More Ideas to Explore

- Try painting with the drill on a flat surface like a table or floor, which is a completely different experience when holding the drill pointing down. Painting on a window or on Plexiglas is another experience to try.

- Experiment with other art tools placed in a drill, like markers, chalk, or crayons. The advantage of a paintbrush is that it does not break easily.

Runaway Sheets, pages 116-117
Sheets photography Barbara Zaborowski
© Bright Ring Publishing 2014

5

Up
Down
All Around

I Am a Vacuum

Young artists enjoy the challenge of using a drinking straw to pick up a scrap of paper, just like a vacuum cleaner! They carry the scrap a short distance to the sticky art canvas where they release the paper scrap, creating a breathtaking paper collage.

Most children's art with straws requires blowing air OUT. This activity works by sucking IN like a vacuum. My preschoolers were captivated by holding their breath as they moved paper from the scrap collection to the sheet of sticky art paper. Art involving use of the body in new or unusual way develops skill and inspires creativity.   ~ BBZ

Materials

- Small scraps of paper (tear into pieces before the activity)
  Note: Art tissue scraps are light and easy to work with.

- Tray, box, or tub to hold paper scraps

- Drawing paper

- White glue thinned with water in a shallow dish, and paintbrushes for painting and stirring

- Drinking straw (one for each artist, label name with permanent marker)

Vacuum photography Barbara Zaborowski © Bright Ring Publishing 2014

Action Process

1. Place a sheet of drawing paper on the table. Taping the paper to the table for stability is helpful, but is not required.

2. Mix white glue with water in the dish, stirring with a paintbrush to thin, and place this beside the drawing paper.

3. A few feet away, place the tray filled with small scraps of paper. The tray can be moved later if it is too far or too close, which can be determined when the project begins.

4. Ready for the action? First paint the drawing paper with thinned white glue, covering the surface to make it sticky.

5. The artist begins at the tray of paper scraps, placing the straw end on a scrap of paper. The artist sucks air into the straw. Artists like to hear someone say, "Turn on the vacuum cleaner!" The paper will be held in place with the suction, but will only hold as long as the artist is breathing "in," which is part of the challenge and fun! (Note: Some artists will carry more than one piece of paper at a time. One piece or many – it all works!)

6. Before breathing "out" (turning "off" the vacuum cleaner), quickly move to the sticky paper, all the while keeping suction on the paper scrap. Bring the scrap to the sticky paper, release it, and let it fall. It will stick in place (a little pat will help). The collage has begun!

7. Repeat the suction and carrying process, bringing more and more scraps to the collage. Hint: Sometimes glue must be refreshed on the paper if it starts to dry out.

8. When the collage feels right, paint a final layer of thinned glue over the entire collage and it will dry shiny and smooth.

The vacuum collage has just begun, as artists add colored paper, scraps, textures, and shapes one by one.

More Ideas to Explore

- Most very young artists can't hold their breath long enough to carry a piece of paper. However, they enjoy hand-tossing paper scraps in the air over sticky paper and letting pieces fall and stick, patting pieces into place by hand.

- Using contact paper, clear or patterned, peel the covering back to expose the sticky surface. Artists press paper scraps or collage items to the sticky area.

Cotton Ball Toss

Explore tossing paint-dipped cotton balls at a large sheet of paper. What works best? Standing close or far away? Hefty throws or gentle tosses?

An outdoor fence is the perfect easel for this artist's active art adventure tossing paint-dipped cotton balls at large paper.

 It seems we spend a good deal of time asking kids not to throw things inside. It's liberating for a parent or teacher to say to an artist, "Yes, you may throw these. In fact, throw as many as you like!"

The photos show a young artist throwing painted cotton balls as far and as hard as he can. Before long, he was happy to have others join in the creative fun. ~ BBZ

Materials

- Big sheet of paper (butcher paper, the back of old wrapping paper, newspaper, cardboard, poster board)
- Cotton balls (inexpensive makeup balls)
- Tempera paint (washable tempera is easiest to cleanup)
- Containers for paint (small paper cups or grocery trays)
- 2 tarps, shower curtains, or plastic table covers
- Clips or tape
- Fence, big sheet of cardboard, or wall

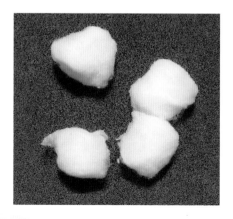

Action ART © 2015 Bright Ring Publishing

Action Process

1. Set up the tarps, one upright and one at the base of the paper to protect the floor or grass. A fence or big sheet of cardboard makes a good support. Rule of thumb: The younger the painter, the wider the protection.

2. Clip or tape the paper to the upright tarp.

3. Suggestion: First practice tossing wet cotton balls without paint to determine a good throwing distance and get the general idea.

4. Pour paint into containers, one color for each. Start with less paint, and add more as needed.

5. Dip a cotton ball in paint using pincer fingers. Get ready, aim, and toss the cotton ball at the paper. About four or five feet away is far enough. Very young children will need to be closer.

Cotton ball photography Barbara Zaborowski © Bright Ring Publishing 2014

Some cotton balls, like the one to the left, will slide off the paper to the ground. Reuse the fallen ones by redipping them in paint, and then ... toss again!

More Ideas to Explore

- **Easel:** Place a cup of clean cotton balls beside cups of paint. Dip cotton balls in paint and press on the easel paper to stick or to make strokes and designs.
- **Shoe box:** Place paper in a shoe box. Drop in a few cotton balls, each dipped in a different color of paint. Put the lid on the box and shake!

Bubble Wrap Boots

Bubble Wrap boots are made for more than walking! Artists explore jumping, hopping, dancing, and marching – all while making noisy popping prints on paper.

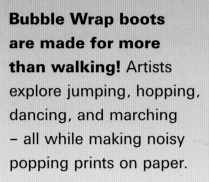

When this young art adventurer put on her bubble boots, she stepped into magenta and purple paint and made tracks from walking, tiptoeing, and some pretty serious hopping. She loved making the Bubble Wrap pop while she experimented with different ways to create colorful footprints on big white paper.   ~ MAK

All Bubble Wrap boot photography, Vicky Perreault 2014, Owner, messforless.net

Materials

- Butcher paper or other large paper
- Scissors, tape
- Tempera paint, two colors
- Paper plates (or grocery trays)
- Paintbrush
- Bubble Wrap
- Old towel or rags

Bubble Wrap boots bring out the smiles!

Action Process

1. Roll butcher paper out on the floor. Then roll another length next to the first. Tape them together. Tape them to the floor too. Choose two colors of paint and pour one color on one paper plate, and one on the other. Place these next to the paper. Give each plate of color a paintbrush.

2. Bubble Wrap Boots: Cut Bubble Wrap wide enough to make a boot to loosely wrap around the artist's bare foot. Tape the Bubble Wrap to hold. There are no specific directions for this – just wrap and tape the Bubble Wrap so both feet are covered.

3. An adult and child together can paint the bottom of each foot. Keep an old towel handy if needed.

4. Ready for the Bubble Wrap painting action? Walk on the paper with the painted Bubble Wrapped feet! Some artists like to jump or hop to get the most out of the popping Bubble Wrap. Marching is another popular choice.
Note: Though slipping or falling doesn't happen very often, children should be supervised during their art experience.

5. Add more paint to boots as needed. Try standing on the paper plates instead of painting on more paint with a brush. It all works!

Tiptoe. Run. Dance. Twist. Walk. Every move makes a footprint, and the popping bubbles sound – and feel! – creative and fun!

More Ideas to Explore
- Make handprints with Bubble Wrap mittens.
- Consider making prints with Bubble Wrap arms, knees, and so on.
- Place Bubble Wrap on the workspace. Tape corners to hold it in place. Paint it with tempera paints. Then press a piece of paper on the Bubble Wrap to lift a print. Did someone press hard enough to pop the bubbles?

Big Arm Action Canvas

When artists have a huge canvas to work on, they can really let loose and use their biggest arm movements and widest-reaching body stretching to cover the surface. Use large house-painting brushes, brushes on poles, and rollers for the most active application of color.

Wall brush painting photography Tanya Hofbauer 2014

Materials

- Open wall or large paper on a wall
- Sidewalk paint, Bio-Colors or washable tempera paints
- Liquid starch, optional
- Variety of brushes: house-painting brushes with handles, sponge brushes, rollers, brushes or sponges on poles, and sponge mops
- Paint pans or plastic containers to fit the size of the brushes
- Buckets of water for rinsing
- Scrub brushes and sponges, rags, old towels, mops, soapy water in buckets
- Tarp, optional

Tanya Hofbauer hung large paper on the wall and left it there all week. The children started working on it with markers, then eventually switched to paint. Max would ask several times a day for "more paint." The "long-term painting" is now a brown-yellow board displayed in her entry. ~ TH

Wall painting dots photography Lakisha Reid 2014, Discovery Early Learning Center

Action Process

1. Head outdoors to the large wall that will be the painting canvas. (If an indoor wall is used, protect the floor by covering with a tarp.) Pour paint into containers big enough for the tools to dip into easily. Start with a shallow amount of paint and add more as needed. Adding liquid starch to the paint will extend the color and make it shinier. Adding water will thin the paint and extend use.

   Note about a group activity: Talk with the group about the painting space before they begin. They can mark off individual sections, or they can agree to move about and paint any surface, including painting over someone else's paint. Also decide with them if this is an exploratory painting experience or if it has a theme to which everyone contributes.

2. Select a brush and begin to paint. Artists will stretch and jump high, squat and bend low, stretch and reach far and wide. Before long, the wall canvas will be filled. All the wonderful choices of brushes will inspire different kinds of movements and applications.

3. Depending on the wall, the painting may remain; or more likely, it will be necessary to wash it away within a few days. To clean the wall, fill buckets with soap and water, hand out brushes, mops, and rags, and everyone helps scrub the wall. Hose rinsing is a big favorite!

Wall rolling paint photography Lakisha Reid 2014, Discovery Early Learning Center

More Ideas to Explore

- Tape an old king-sized bedsheet securely to a large surface like a wall or floor. Allow kids to use long or large paint tools that will reach into the center of the sheet so they can paint the entire sheet. A random design or a planned design can be used (plan ahead with the artists).
- Permanent markers can be used when the fabric is dry to enhance the painting.

Paint in Motion

Discover the different strokes that result from running, jumping, twirling, and marching past a long piece of paper taped to a fence or wall.

Materials

- Tempera paints and easel brushes (wide-tip brushes work better than thin)
- Cups, bowls, or other containers
- Long piece of paper 6'-8' (3'-4' is fine)

- Suitable area to hang the paper: fence, large piece of cardboard, wall
- Tape or stapler for hanging paper
- Tarp for protection, if needed
- Buckets of water for rinsing, old towels

Motion photography Barbara Zaborowski © Bright Ring Publishing 2014

My preschoolers love playing the MOVE & PAINT card game with the suspense of finding out what motion they will be using to paint the big paper. Some action words are new to some of them, like *twirl* or *tremble*. There are always artists who like to contribute new words to the game. One artist wanted to paint like a giraffe (*giraffing?*) with the brush held high overhead. Creativity is just plain fun at times!   ~ BBZ

Preschoolers enjoy playing the Move & Paint card game. The artist's motion card (above left) said "jump." Her hair confirms it!

The artist's motion card (above right) was "backward," a challenging movement for painting the canvas on the fence.

Action ART © 2015 Bright Ring Publishing

Action Process

1. Clip or staple the long paper on the fence, cardboard, or wall at child height. Set out four or five colors of paint in bowls or cups.

2. The artist chooses a color, dipping the brush in the paint, and filling it well.

3. Next the artist decides which movement to use to apply the paint. Some ideas are: run, hop, skip, twirl, march, walk backward, dance, swim, or tiptoe. Artists will have more word-motion ideas.
   Note: Don't be surprised to hear terms like karate, Superman, or bunny. Swimming the breaststroke will mean painting backward while moving forward. Try it!

4. Picture this: If the artist runs, she will run past the paper, applying the paint while passing by. If hopping, the artist hops by the paper applying paint while hopping by. Each time an artist passes by the paper, paint will be applied with the chosen movement. Hint: Some artists like to try more than one movement! A group of artists will have much to explore as they take turns applying paint in chosen motions.

5. When the painting is done, artists may enjoy trying to guess which paint strokes were made with which movements.

If you guessed the motion word was "run," you guessed correctly.

More Ideas to Explore
Move & Paint, a card game

- Create a game by picking a card from a small deck of movement possibility cards. Each card will say one word, or show a picture of one movement, like *run, hop, dance*. Artists often like the suspense and fun of letting the card dictate the painting movement. Kids always want to think up new movement cards to add to the game.

Dancing Blottos

Blottos are a basic art experience for children where a piece of paper is painted, folded in half, and rubbed to spread the paint outwards, making a double design. Now enter Dancing Blottos, a full-body action art experience! Bring on the dancing music!

Put on those dancing bread bags to cover shoes.

Materials

- Tarp to protect the ground or floor
- Large sheets of paper
- Tempera paints in picnic squirt bottles
- Large paintbrushes
- Protection for clothes and shoes (or wear art clothes)
- Dancing music of choice, optional

The anticipation of opening a folded piece of paper to see what was created is so exciting! That's what kids love about "blottos" (or whatever you call them). But in this case, the results were unseated by the sheer fun of dancing on the artwork with friends. Music wasn't even needed! A reminder: Children love to dance!
~ BBZ

Blotto photography Barbara Zaborowski © Bright Ring Publishing 201

Action Process

1. Artists should wear art clothes or protect their clothes and shoes before beginning. Spread out a tarp so there will be enough room to fit under the art and cover it.

2. Fill picnic squirt bottles about half-full of tempera paints, one squirt bottle per color. If you don't have picnic squirt bottles, save shampoo or lotion bottles to use for squirting paint.

3. Place a large sheet of paper on top of one half of the tarp. Squirt several colors of paint on the paper.

4. Fold the paper in half. Now pull the other half of the tarp over the folded paper to cover it completely.

5. The artist, along with any friends, dances on the tarp and the folded paper beneath the tarp. Dance and enjoy moving. Add music for inspiration.

6. When the dancing is over, pull back the tarp and unfold the paper to see the all-new big blottos created with dancing feet.

More Ideas to Explore

- An adult may control the music, deciding when to start and stop, to keep an eye on the painted paper so it is not danced to shreds.
- Rolling Body Blottos are another way to involve the action of the body in painting. Roll back and forth across the tarp several times instead of dancing.

Getting started with purple paint puddles.

Jump-It Squirt Paint

Get the body into action! Fill picnic squeeze bottles with liquid watercolors.

Then jump, stomp, step, tap, and tromp to create puddles, sprays, splatters, and squirts of abstract art. Choose a work area that is adequately prepared to be worry-free, where artistic freedom can bloom and show amazing impressive artwork.

Materials

- Paper, large
- Tarp, shower curtain, newspaper, or other cover
- Protection for shoes (suggest newspaper sleeves or plastic bags pulled over shoes)
- Picnic squeeze bottles, one for each color (suggest plastic ketchup and mustard squeeze bottles from the dollar store)
- Liquid watercolors
- Outdoor work area recommended, or spacious indoor work area
- Tape, optional

Squeeze the squirt bottle carefully, or jump with full action! Every painting style inspires new learning. Notice the beads of squirting orange paint in the photo below. Hint: Bread bags make perfect shoe covers!

Artists love to get their bodies actively involved in art, and this one invites kids to jump in and give paint a new trajectory with unique results. The kids were lining up for turns, which doesn't always happen. Be prepared for very wet art that will dry overnight.   ~ BBZ

Squirt photography Barbara Zaborowski © Bright Ring Publishing 201

Action ART © 2015 Bright Ring Publishing

Action Process

1. Spread out the tarp or other cover. Place the large paper in the center of the cover. Several large sheets can be taped together to make an even larger canvas. The paint can really travel, so cover anything near the activity that needs protection from spatters. Artists should cover their shoes, or wear art shoes that are worry free. Artists can work individually, as partners, or as a small group.

2. Pour liquid watercolors in the squeeze bottles.

3. Now for the action! To begin, place one squeeze bottle on its side at the edge of the paper.

4. Stomp on the bottle with one foot, propelling paint onto the paper. Don't be shy!

5. Change paint and the bottle position at any time. Note: If it is impractical to move the bottles around the paper, leave the bottles where they are, and instead, turn the paper.

6. If possible, let the art dry in place. Liquid watercolors dry fairly fast. Otherwise, be prepared to move the art to a large drying area.

More Ideas to Explore

• Very young artists can easily work with squeeze bottles filled with clear water and create water designs on dry pavement. These will dry quickly, leaving room to create more and more designs.

• To achieve artful puddles of paint, enthusiastic jumping and stomping work wonders. Very wet art should be left in place to dry. The puddles mix and blend and dry with a very different effect than sprays, squirts, and splatters.

Runaway Sheets

Tearing a painted bedsheet into strips and weaving them through a fence combines favorite activities of most kids: running, tearing, laughing, decorating, and making noise.

My active preschoolers love to run with the sound of the tearing sheet following them. Later, when the strips have been painted, weaving the fence is full of fun mixed with serious creative focus.

~ BBZ

Materials

- Bedsheets or similar-sized fabric (available from thrift stores)
- Scissors
- Liquid watercolors in small containers or shallow jar lids
- Paintbrushes, variety of sizes
- Container of water for rinsing brushes, old towel or rags
- Tape, optional
- Fence, if available

More Ideas for Creating with Torn Strips

- Paint on the strips with eyedroppers, pipettes, misting bottles, or spray bottles.
- Draw on the strips with markers or fabric crayons.
- Tie 3 or 4 strips to one shower curtain ring to make "dancing ribbons."
- Make a hanging sculpture by tying strips to a Hula-Hoop; hang the hoop from the ceiling (or over the artist's bed at home). Embroidery hoops are another option.
- Strips can be tied to clothes hangers and hung about the room, on the porch in the breeze, or over a door to make a fancy entry.
- Use as ribbons to tie around gifts.
- Tie strips to a curtain rod to make a curtain.
- Simply weave them, braid them, tie them together – no need for any display area, fence, rings, or hangers.

Artists like the girl to the left are in perfect harmony as they discover the sound and feel of tearing art sheets.

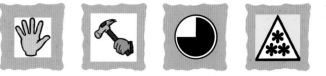

Action Process

1. Make 4"-5" long snips along one edge of the sheet, about 2"-3" apart. The artist holds tightly to one cut piece and a partner or an adult stabilizes the rest of the sheet, holding tightly.

2. When ready, the artist starts running, pulling the torn piece of sheet along behind. The tearing of the sheet will be significantly noisy! Often the last inch or so of the sheet will need to be cut with scissors because of a hem that won't tear.

3. To decorate the torn strip, lay it out on a covered workspace. Tape edges down, if you wish, to keep the strip from moving about. Paint directly on the torn strip with liquid watercolors.

4. When the strip has dried some, take it to the fence and weave it in. Tying strips together, braiding, and other techniques will emerge.
   Note: If a fence is not available, a large sheet of cardboard with holes poked in it will work great.

Sheets photography Barbara Zaborowski © Bright Ring Publishing 2014

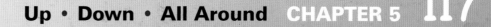

Helmet Painting

A bicycle helmet is the perfect tool to accommodate a large paintbrush, and the artist's head must do the work of painting without hands. Painting with one's head is a whole body action activity and a big favorite of artists who enjoy a challenge!

Materials

- Bicycle helmet (recycled for art use only). Note: A soft hat or baseball hat won't work, but a hard hat will.
- Tempera paints
- Brushes, the bigger the better
- Paper, any kind, preferably large
- Upright easel or other surface
- Wide-mouthed containers, big enough to dip big brushes (half-gallon milk cartons cut down to 6" or so work well)
- Duct tape
- Tub or bucket of water for rinsing brushes, old towel or rags

Artists who have done many process art activities are often ready and willing for whatever art challenge and experience they can dream up. In this case, it's painting with their heads, not their hands. Not easy! The artists were delighted. ~ BBZ

Close-up of helmet and brush

Tape a wide paintbrush to an old bike helmet. Artists paint with their heads instead of hands.

Action Process

1. Attach the paper to the easel or upright surface. Tape the containers of paint to the workspace so they won't tip over. Attach the brushes to the helmet with duct tape. Attach one brush on the top of the helmet or one on each side of the hat. It's fun to have several helmets ready to go with different brush arrangements from which artists may choose.

2. The artist puts on a helmet and tightens the chin strap. If the helmet is wiggly or loose, the artist may steady the helmet by holding the sides.

3. The action begins as the artist bends over and dips one of the brushes in paint. Note: Some artists like to "pre-paint" the helmet's brushes rather than dipping them.

4. The artist turns his or her head and moves his or her whole body to paint with the brushes attached to the helmet. Artists usually have to steady the helmet with both hands while painting. Squatting, jumping, and side-to-side movements are encouraged!

5. When the helmet is removed, the artist can rinse the brush without removing the duct tape. The clean brush will be ready for the next artist.

Helmet photography Barbara Zaborowski © Bright Ring Publishing 2014

More Ideas to Explore

- Tape a brush to the top of the helmet with the bristles facing backward (see above). The artist should stand with his or her back toward the paper to paint. Some assistance may be needed.

- Helmet Bubble Prints: Cover a helmet with Bubble Wrap. Hold on to the helmet, and dip or press the Bubble Wrap onto a tray of paint (or paint directly on the Bubble Wrap with a brush). Press the bubble-wrapped helmet on paper to make prints. Change colors anytime.

Plexi Friendship Paint

Invite viewing a friend's face on the other side of the see-through easel, in a new way.
Take the time to build a simple Plexiglas easel, and the opportunities for art will fascinate and inspire children with many new experiences. Numerous ideas for building Plexiglas easels can be found on the Internet so you can choose one that works for your budget and needs.

Painting a friend's face without touching is fun and new for most artists. The kids in these photos were happy taking turns being Painter or Model. Generally, Models acted quite silly and Painters were more serious. ~ MAK

Materials

- Build a Plexi-Easel: rectangle of Plexiglas, boards, plywood, nails, and hammer – or – screws and screw driver (Easy idea: Remove the regular easel boards from the paint easel, and secure a sheet – or two sheets – of clear Plexiglas to the easel instead.)
- Paintbrushes, any kind (foam brushes are easy for young artists to handle)
- Washable tempera paints in non-tipping containers like Bio-Colors (cut down milk cartons are good non-tip containers)
- Cleanup: spray bottles with clear water, old towels (small bucket of water and a sponge are another good choice)
- Box to hold paints
- Friends

Shadow Plexiglas photography Peggy Ashbrook 2014

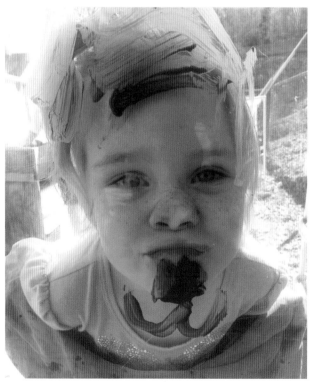

Plexiglas photography Barbara Zaborowski © Bright Ring 2014

Action Process

1. Set the containers of tempera paints in a box on the ground next to the easel. The box will help keep the paints from tipping over. Arrange the clear water and cleaning supplies in another box nearby.

2. Two artists stand, each on one side of the easel. The artist who will be first to paint looks through the clear easel, and the other artist places her face near the clear plastic. The friend who is not painting may be making funny faces!

3. The artist begins to paint on the clear plastic, painting around the friend's features. Both artists should find the process intriguing and interesting!

4. Get ready to switch places, but first, cleanup. Wash the Plexiglas. Wipe dry.

5. Now the artists trade places and repeat the painting activity.

Easy-Build Plexi-Easel

Purchase a large rectangle of Plexiglas from a home improvement store or other vendor. Then create a base for the Plexiglas rectangle with two boards nailed together that will fit on the bottom of a short side of the Plexiglas rectangle. Add legs or a foot for the base with boards or plywood screwed in place. The Plexi-Easel will look something like a standing mirror. Idea: A preschool we visited nailed their Plexiglas rectangle in a doorway that was rarely used – kids painted from both sides.

Check out this doable DIY Plexiglas easel from The Play at Home Mom:
http://www.playathomemomllc.com/2011/06/money-saving-tips-and-building-your-own-furniture/

More Ideas to Explore

- Both artists can paint at the same time.
- Fingerpaint on the Plexiglas.
- Lift a print by patting a sheet of paper on the painting and then peeling off.
- Paint on a window. Washable paint works great!

Funnel Painting, Photography 2014 Claudia Chamberland

Resource Guide

ART Collage Materials to Save

A
acorns
allspice
almonds
aluminum foil
apple seeds
apricot seeds

B
baking cups
balsa wood
bamboo skewers
bark
basket reeds
beads
beans
belts
bias tape
blotter paper
bobby pins
bolts and nuts
bones
bottle caps
bottles
boxes
brads
burlap scraps
buttons

C
cancelled stamps
candles, small birthday
candy sprinkles
candy wrappers
cardboard scraps
cards
carpet samples
cellophane scraps
cellophane tape
chains
chalk
checkers
chopsticks

clothespins
cloth scraps
cloves
coffee filters
coffee grounds
coins
combs
confetti
construction paper scraps
contact paper
cord
corks
corn husks
corn kernels
cotton
cotton balls
craft foam
craft crystals
crayon shavings
crepe paper

D
dice
doilies
dominoes
drapery samples
dried beans and peas
dried flowers
dried grass
dried seeds
driftwood
dry cereals

E
Easter grass
egg cartons
eggshells
elastic
emery boards
embroidery hoop
embroidery floss, thread
evergreens
eyelets
excelsior

F
fabric scraps
fasteners
faucet washers
feathers
felt scraps
film cartridges
film spools
filters, coffee
fish tank gravel
fishing lures
flashbulbs
flocking
florist foil, foam, tape
flowers
flowers, artificial
flowers, dried
flowers, plastic
foam packing
fur, faux

G
game pieces, cards
gauze
gift wrap, tags
glass mosaic pieces
glitter
googly eyes
gold thread
grains
gravel
greeting cards
gummed labels
gummed reinforcements
gummy candies

H
hair netting
hairpins
hair rollers
hardware scraps
hat trimmings
holiday decorations

I
ice cream stick
ice cream spoons, wood
inner tube scraps

J
jewelry pieces
jewelry wire
junk of all kinds
junk mail
jute

K
key rings
key tabs
keys

L
labels
lace
laminated items
leather scraps
leaves
lentils
lids
linoleum scraps

M
macaroni, pasta noodles
magazine clippings
mailing tubes
map pins
marbles
masonite
matte frames
meat trays, paper
meat trays, plastic
metal shavings
mirrors
mosaic squares, tiles
mosquito netting
moss, dried

ART Collage Materials

Action ART © 2015 Bright Ring Publishing

Safety Reminder: Please carefully supervise
children at all times while using collage materials.

. . . .

N

nails
napkins
newspaper
noodles (pasta), dry
noodles, wet
nut cups
nuts & seeds

O

oilcloth scraps
orange seeds
origami paper
ornaments

P

packing peanuts
paint chips
paper baking cups
paper clips
paper dots
paper fasteners
paper products, all
paper towel tubes
parchment paper
pasta, dry
peanuts, peanut shells
pebbles
photos
pinecones
pine needles
pipe cleaners
plastic, all kinds
plastic bottles
plastic foam
plastic wrap
pom-poms
popcorn
Popsicle sticks
postcards
pumpkin seeds
puzzle pieces

Q

Q-tips (cotton buds)
quills
quinoa

R

raffia
rhinestones
ribbon
rice
rickrack
rock salt
rocks
rope
rubber bands
rubber tubing

S

safety pins
salt
sand
sandpaper
sawdust
scouring pads
scrapbooking papers
screen, plastic or wire
screws
seals, gummed
seam binding
seashells
seedpods
seeds
sequins
sewing tape
shells
shoelaces
shot
silk scraps
skewers, bamboo
skewers, wooden
soap
soldering wire
spaghetti, pasta dry

sponges
spools
spray can lids
stamps, all kinds
stars, bummer
steel wool
sticks
stickers
sticky dots
stones
straws, broom
straws, drinking
straws, stirring
streamers
string
Styrofoam

T

tape, cellophane
tape, duct
tape, library
tape, masking
tape, mystic
tape, plastic
tape, Scotch
tape, sewing
tape, washi
telephone wire
thistles
thread
tiles
Tinkertoy parts
tinsel
tissue paper
tongue depressors
toothpicks
torn paper scraps
twigs
twine

U

umbrellas, paper/party
used items, variety

V

Valentines

W

wallpaper
warp
washers
washi tape
wax paper
weeds
wire
wood blocks
wood craft sticks
wood scraps
wood shavings
wooden beads
wooden dowels
wool
wrapping paper

X

X-rays, pictures of

Y

yarn
yogurt lids, foil

Z

zippers
ziplock bags

*Collage list excerpt printed with
permission from SCRIBBLE ART (Bright
Ring Publishing, Inc.),1994, Bright Ideas
for Learning series, MaryAnn F. Kohl
author, pps. 152-153.*

Some ARTSY Internet Visits

Listed here are artsy blogs, websites, and social media pages that are just some of our many favorite places to find process art and action art activities with their clear photos and helpful hints.

Art Bar
artbarblog.com
Bar Rucci's blog encourages us to find our inner artist by providing kids with simple ways to express & problem-solve.
facebook.com/artbarblog

Art for Small Hands
artforsmallhands.com
Julie Voigt guides how to instruct & develop art without dampening the artist in every child.

The Artful Parent
artfulparent.com
Jean Van't Hul shares simple ways to fill your family's life with art & creativity.

Babble Dabble Do
babbledabbledo.com
Anna Louisa Dziengel's blog is a chronicle of activities for imaginative families.

Barbara Zaborowski
barbarazab.tumblr.com
Barbara Zaborowski shares process art from Shadow Rock Preschool in Phoenix.

Blog Me Mom
blogmemom.com
Suja and Deepa share fun art, science, math, & creative activities.
facebook.com/blogmemom

Casa Maria's Creative Learning Zone
casamarias.blogspot.com
Maria Wynne believes in imagination, dreams, & adventures (also on Facebook).

Child Central Station
childcentralstation.com/blog
Amy Ahola believes in learning through play. She asks, "Just playing?" and answers her question in inspiring ways.
amyahola.com & facebook.com/ChildCentralStation

Childhood 101
childhood101.com
Christie Burnett offers play, learning, & creativity with activities, projects, & ideas; food & family time; positive parenting; home & garden. facebook.com/Childhood101

The Chocolate Muffin Tree
thechocolatemuffintree.blogspot.com
Melissa Jordan shares inspiration to be creative with children!

Creative Play Central
blog.creativeplaycentral.com.au/
Elise Ellerman creates original creative opportunities for children to play, create & learn.

Dirt and Boogers
dirtandboogers.com
Amanda Reuter gives process art ideas & photos to share.
facebook.com/DirtAndBoogers

Deep Space Sparkle
deepspacesparkle.com/blog
Patty Palmer offers art lessons, lesson plans, & resources to make art with kids easier.

Filth Wizardry
filthwizardry.com
Lindsey Boardman shares messy art & craft activities for kids & much more.

Fun at Home with Kids
funathomewithkids.com
Asia Citro offers a range of science, art, crafts, sensory play, & small world play.

Gingerbread Lane Play House
facebook.com/gingerbreadlanefamilydaycare
Inspiring projects of all kinds are here from Leisha Harrelson.

Hand Made Kid's Art
handmadekidsart.com
facebook.com/handmadekidsart
Jamie Hand shares art projects for the busy family, quick on time & easy on cleanup.

Happy Hooligans
happyhooligans.ca
Jackie Currie's blog is dedicated to easy affordable art, crafts, & old-fashioned play.
facebook.com/happyhooligansblog

The Homegrown Preschooler
homegrownpreschooler.com
Kathy Lee & Lesli Richards offer creativity & skillful play for preschoolers where they live.

Imagination Soup
imaginationsoup.net
Melissa Taylor features inspiration for literacy, learning, & thinking.

Want more ideas? Take a look at art museums that often have specific sites just for kids. Hint: Many art-filled websites and blogs have the same name on Facebook with even more ideas to share!

Let us know YOUR favorites, and we'll update a list for you at www.brightring.com.

You are warmly invited to join *Process Art with MaryAnn Kohl* at facebook.com/groups/processart.

The Imagination Tree
theimaginationtree.com
  Anna Ranson has excellent creative ideas! Click on "creativity" under the "activities" menu.

Interaction Imagination
facebook.com/InteractionImagination
  Susanne Axelsson posts art & more with Reggio Emilia inspiration.

Kids Activities Blog
kidsactivitiesblog.com
  Holly Homer inspires fun & frugal activities (with Rachel Miller, formerly of Quirky Momma).

Messy Hands and Lesson Plans
messyhandslessonplans.com
  Amanda Sipple shares open-ended art ideas.

My Nearest and Dearest
mynearestanddearest.com/tag/process-art
  Ann Harquail posts excellent process art ideas.

Not Just Cute
notjustcute.com
  Amanda Morgan shares tidbits of research, philosophy, resources, & activities.

Nurture Store
facebook.com/NurtureStore
Cathy James shares 1,000+ kids' activities ideas, free printables, & super ebooks.
nurturestore.co.uk

One Time Through
onetimethrough.com
  Sue Lively's sensory link includes process art & open-ended crafts.

Paint Cut Paste
paintcutpaste.com
  Jen Berlingo stresses child-centered, process-oriented exploration & expression in art.

Picklebums
picklebums.com
  Kate likes sharing family recipes, kids' activities, conversations about parenting & free printables.

Pink and Green Mama
pinkandgreenmama.blogspot.com
  MaryLea Harris has creative ideas for toddlers, preschoolers, & school age children.

Play at Home Mom
playathomemomllc.com
  Ashley Kagen & Rosie Lamphere believe children are competent & capable; learn through play; are our best teachers.

Play-Based Learning
playbasedlearning.com.au
  Sherry Hutton & Donna Ridley give irresistible ideas for play-based learning .

Process Art with MaryAnn Kohl
facebook.com/groups/processart
  MaryAnn Kohl's process art Facebook group is active with daily process art ideas and photos.

Red Ted Art
redtedart.com
  Maggy Woodley brings color & art to children.

Teacher Tom
teachertomsblog.blogspot.com
  Tom Hobson works very closely with families at his preschool, & uses open, creative ideas.

TinkerLab
tinkerlab.com
  Rachelle Doorley inspires ways to raise confident & creative thinkers through child-directed process projects.
facebook.com/tinkerlab

Tiny Rotten Peanuts & Artchoo
tinyrottenpeanuts.com
  Jeanette Nyberg shares kids' art ideas, craft projects, design for kids, & inspiration for life with kids to be super-creative.
facebook.com/Artchooblog

Online Interactive Art Sites
permadi.com/java/spaint/spaint.html
  Make kaleidoscope images.

artpad.art.com/artpad/painter
  Choose colors, tools, sizes, and more.

picassohead.com/create.html
  Create Picasso-like heads.

weavesilk.com
  Create silky, kaleidoscopic art.

jacksonpollock.org
  Create Pollock-style paintings.

ARTISTS in Action Scrapbook

Six scrapbook pages share photos of kids in action and their process art. Notice the focus in their expressions! Feel their creativity! Be inspired! And enjoy.

Kids experiment with block prints. (Zannifer Rolich)

Fingerpainting is always new. (Leisha Harrelson)

Spin a top in paint puddles. (Gill Robertson)

Painting with toy cars creates tracks. (Leisha Harrelson)

Babies explore clay. (Claudia Chamberland)

Pound paint on paper plates under a clear shower curtain. (Barbara Zaborowski)

Action ART © 2015 Bright Ring Publishing

Photography credits are shown within parentheses beneath each photograph.

Think left and think right and think low and think high.
Oh, the thinks you can think up if only you try.
— Dr. Seuss

Paint-covered hands offer much to consider. (Alison Gall)

Designs on a shiny CD. (Robertson)

Kids paint with baby bottles. (Gill Robertson)

Spin art on a record player. (Mrs. O'Connor)

Spatula painting. (Sipple)

"Mrs. O'Connor, I realllly love sewing!" said this usually quiet little artist. (Mrs. O'Connor)

A hand drill is inspiring for art. (Mrs. O'Connor)

Roll a coffee can up an incline with paint-dipped marbles inside to create surprise designs. (Barbara Zaborowski)

The important thing is to create.

– Pablo Picasso

Reveling in *scherenschnitte*! (paper-cutting). (Kohl)

Paper plate twisting delivers a surprise! (Zaborowski)

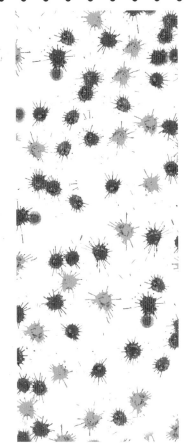

Bingo bottle dots! (Kohl)

Preschoolers are tossing painty cotton balls. (Zaborowski)

Kids paint on a huge wall outdoors. (Lakisha Reid, Discovery Early Learning Center)

Artists can use the whole body to make prints. (Margaret Mahowald)

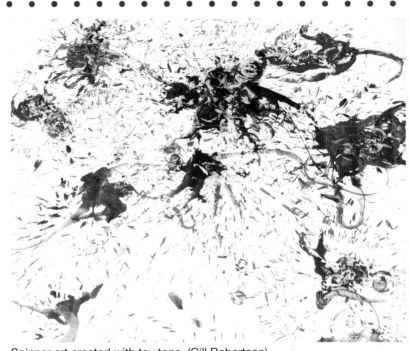

Spinner art created with toy tops. (Gill Robertson)

Exploring wet tissue paper with a rolling pin. (Margaret Mahowald)

Yes, she CAN paint with an electric mixer! (Asia Citro)

Time to explore and discover is important. (Lakisha Reid)

Marker art on the wall. (Tanya Hofbauer)

Pulling a fork through paint is a texture process experience.

Kids squirt paint instead of plain water (above and below). (Shaunna Evans)

Dough changes with each touch. (Zannifer Rolich)

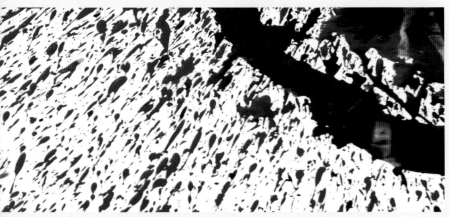

A squirt painting experience emerges in red and blue.

Ice painting is a cool art process. (Claudia Chamberland)

Snow painting (above 3) is all about the process. Pans, bowls, paints, droppers, brushes, and snow inspire exploration and discovery. (Leisha Harrelson)

Squirting paint from the tempera paint bottle is discovered (and encouraged). (Alison Gall)

Artists are never too young to explore, discover, and create. (Gari Stein)

Expressions during creativity. (Leisha Harrelson)

Paint-spattered feet . (Claudia Chamberland)

Paint, feathers, cotton balls, sponge brushes – you name it – all to explore, and all on one table!. (Gari Stein)

Eyedroppers invite experimentation. (Gari Stein)

Painting with funnels. (Claudia Chamberland)

The process and action of eyedroppers and coffee filters is always inspiring. (Ronda Harbaugh)

Action ART Activities

Action ART activities are listed alphabetically to help quickly locate your favorite active process art activities.

Photography Barbara Zaborowski 2014 © Bright Ring, Dancing Blottos, pp.112-113

Photography Tanya Hofbrauer 2014, Big Arm Action Canvas, pp. 108-109

ART Materials Sources

Action ART uses old standbys like tempera paints and glue, as well as less common materials like tires and party blowers. The list suggests where to find more unusual, budget-friendly art materials.

A

ART TISSUE PAPER (BLEEDING, NOT GIFT-WRAP TISSUE)
Craft or hobby stores, Discount School Supply online & other early childhood or art supply sites.

B

BICYCLE HELMET, USED
Garage sales, Goodwill, thrift stores, friends. For art only.

BICYCLE WHEEL
Garage sales & recycle stores. Check bike shops.

BINGO BOTTLES
Discount School Supply & online early childhood & art supply sites, craft & hobby stores. Make your own with a sponge chunk pushed into the opening of a plastic bottle.

C

CHOPSTICKS
Ask restaurant to donate. Save unused from restaurant visits. Restaurant supply sells inexpensive bulk. Dollar stores, grocery stores.

COMPACT DISCS (CDs)
Garage sales, Goodwill, thrift stores, friends. Check with an office or office store for damaged or used.

CONFETTI
Make your own with a hole punch. Ask scrapbooking friends. Tear or chop paper. Buy in bulk from online craft or art supply sites, from early childhood sites,

Discount School Supply, craft & hobby stores. Snip ribbon, doilies, & other materials.

COTTON BALLS
Use inexpensive makeup puffs. Goodwill, thrift stores, garage sales, dollar stores, discount stores. Sterile cotton balls are too costly.

D

DRILL
Borrow (& return) electric or hand-held drills from friends or family. Hardware stores, home stores, Goodwill, thrift stores, garage sales. Ask someone to donate one if it still works safely.

DRINKING STRAWS
Buy in bulk from restaurant supply. Use only new/clean straws if in kids' mouths. General art use (cutting up, etc.), go to Goodwill, garage sales, dollar stores, & thrift stores.

E

EGGBEATER, MANUAL (NOT ELECTRIC)
Many found at Goodwill & thrift stores; also variety of kitchen utensils (whisks, spatulas, basters, & so on).

EYEDROPPERS
Discount School Supply & educational supply sites have kid-style eyedroppers & pipettes. Craft and hobby stores, teacher stores, pharmacies, veterinarians.

F

FOAM BLOCK (OTHER FOAM)
Polystyrene & Styrofoam. From cartons packing appliances, computers, furniture, more. Home stores carry sheets to score & snap/cut. Restaurant supply sell bulk foam products in all shapes & sizes.

G-H-I

GLOVES (LATEX)
Ask a doctor, dentist, pediatrician or restaurant to donate a box or handful. Available at pharmacy, restaurant supply, & home stores.

GOLF TEES
Ask a golf shop or pro shop to donate or save. Driving ranges have used tees. Buy in bulk online. Goodwill, thrift stores, garage sales.

HAIR DRYER (BLOW-DRYER)
Best to use one you know is working safely. Also garage sales, Goodwill, thrift stores, friends. Use for art only.

HULA-HOOP
Garage sales, Goodwill, thrift stores, friends. Make your own with a garden hose section, a piece of dowel to join ends, & duct tape.

M-N-O

MODELING CLAY (PLASTICINE) (NON-HARDENING, COLORFUL)
School supply stores carry quality like Crayola. Discount School Supply's Plasticine by Jovi is highly

recommended. Find other at Walmart, discount stores, Goodwill, thrift and dollar stores. Varying quality.

NEWSPRINT, LARGE ROLLS
Ask a newspaper company to save a wide roll end.

P

PAINT (HINTS ABOUT)
Poster paint and tempera paint are the same thing. Powdered tempera paint mixes with water to make liquid, and is used as a powder for other art explorations. All tempera or acrylic paint can be thinned. Acrylic is more waterproof than tempera. (Try Bio-Color from Discount School Supply: www.discountschoolsupply.com.) Liquid Watercolors are a staple used throughout this book. Can be thinned or colors mixed.

POSTERS (RECYCLE)
Garage sales, Goodwill, thrift stores, friends. Ask print shops for misprints or dented sheets.

Q-R

R/C TOY CARS
Radio controlled cars. Discount stores & dollar stores, Goodwill, thrift stores, garage sales. Ask friends with grown kids to donate.

S-T

SPRAY BOTTLES
Varieties include spray or misting type. Garage sales, Goodwill, thrift

stores, friends. Discount School Supply has child size, high quality.

U-V-W

WHEELS, TIRES
Hardware stores carry tire sizes from stroller up to truck and in between including lawn mower and scooter sizes. Garage sales, Goodwill, thrift stores, service stations, tire stores, friends.

X-Y-Z

ZIPLOCK BAGS
Garage sales, Goodwill, thrift stores, discount stores, restaurant supply stores. Inexpensive varieties at dollar stores.

Photography Robbie Capp 2014

Action ART Index

The *Action ART* Index is a convenient tool for quick searches. Easily search the full list of art materials used throughout the book, activity names, activity extensions, and contributors.

To learn, children must have the opportunity to think. Allow them time to explore, discover, and create.
~ *MaryAnn F. Kohl*

Ronda Harbaugh 2014, Spinning Hanging CDs, pp. 38-39

Barbara Zaborowski 2014 © Bright Ring, Slap Glove Painting, pp. 26-27

Action ART Contributors

Sincere thanks to all the *Action ART* contributors of photography and/or assistance, whose unstaged real-time photos show kids in full natural action creating art. How fortunate the children are to have you to guide their adventures in process art!

Contributors of photography are listed by first name in bold in the page order of the book. Those who supplied a blog or website address are further noted. Some contributors wished to be listed only by blog names, and are noted as requested.

Names without page numbers indicate those whose photography was submitted (so generous!) but not used due to space limitations. Thank you for your generosity and willingness to share for the benefit of children's process art.

> One look at the focused facial expressions of young artists in action convinces me that **process art is vital to child development.**
> ~ MaryAnn Kohl

Thank you all for giving the precious gift of process art to children.

Action ART Authors

MARYANN F. KOHL

MaryAnn Faubion Kohl is the award-winning author of over twenty art books for children, including *Discovering Great Artists*, *Mudworks*, *Scribble Art*, *Preschool Art*, and *First Art*. She is a national presenter, educator, consultant, literary agent, and publisher. MaryAnn's focus on creativity is driven by her passion for children's process art experiences and explorations. MaryAnn enjoys playing outside rain or shine, reading, writing, friends, a morning cup of tea, and most of all, her family. MaryAnn resides in Bellingham, Washington.

BARBARA ZABOROWSKI

Barbara Zaborowski once wished her own children's preschool years would never end, so she began teaching preschool in 1987. Now she has the best of both worlds: two grown children, a new granddaughter, and wonderful years of working with four-to-five-year-olds. Process art has become an important part of her curriculum. She also enjoys friends, reading, the theater, great conversations, and treasure hunts. Despite her best efforts at avoiding extra work, she seems to have become a writer. This is her first book. Barbara lives and works at Shadow Rock Preschool, Phoenix, Arizona.

Bright Ideas Bookshelf · · · · · · · MaryAnn F. Kohl Art Resource Books · *Award Winning*

ACTION ART
Hands-On Active Art Adventures

MaryAnn Kohl & Barbara Zaborowski

ISBN 9780935607345

Over 100 art experiences involving active participaton by kids 2-12. Ride a bike through paint! Make plunger prints! Catapult painty cotton balls! Rake chalk design! Five chapters include rolling, spinning, smooshing, and much more.

**$21.95 • 144 pages
Bright Ring • 2015
Ages 2-12**

STORYBOOK ART
Hands-On Art for Children in the Styles of 100 Great Picture Book Illustrators

MaryAnn Kohl & Jean Potter

ISBN 9780935607031

100 easy literature based art ideas in the styles of favorite picture book illustrators. Preschool through elementary. Extensive indexes and info.

**$18.95 • 144 pages
Bright Ring • 2003
Ages 4-12**

SCIENCE ARTS
Discovering Science Through Art Experiences

MaryAnn F. Kohl & Jean Potter

ISBN 9780935607048

200+ art experiences explore basic science concepts. Amazing *ooo-ahh* projects entice even the most reluctant artist into exploration, discovery, and creativity. Projects worthy of repeating over and over.

**$18.95 • 144 pages
Bright Ring • 1993
Ages 3-10**

GOOD EARTH ART
Environmental Art for Kids

MaryAnn Kohl & Cindy Gainer

ISBN 9780935607017

200+ art explorations using common materials collected from nature or recycled from throw-aways. Fllled with easy ideas for appreciating the earth through art.

**$18.95 • 224 pages
Bright Ring • 1991
Ages 4-10**

Great Masters Series

DISCOVERING GREAT ARTISTS
Hands-On Art for Children in the Styles of the Great Masters

MaryAnn Kohl & Kim Solga

ISBN 9780935607093

100+ easy art ideas with the style of great masters, past and present. More than 80 artists featured including Picasso, Monet, & O'Keeffe. Highly accaimed book with numerous awards including Benjamin Franklin and Homeschooling.

**$18.95 • 144 pages
Bright Ring • 1996
Ages 3-12**

GREAT AMERICAN ARTISTS FOR KIDS
Hands-On Art Experiences in the Styles of Great American Masters

MaryAnn Kohl & Kim Solga

ISBN 9780935607000

75+ open-ended art ideas focus on the styles of great American masters from colonial times to the present. Full color artworks by masters and children! Young child art options included. Some are Cassatt, Wood, Warhol, Kahn, Hopper, Neiman, Lin, Fish, Chihuly, Hofmann, Stuart, Johns.

**$18.95 • 144 pages
Bright Ring • 2008
Ages 4-12**

SCRIBBLE ART
Independent Creative Art Experiences for Children

MaryAnn Kohl

ISBN 9780935607055

200+ process art ideas that applaud exploring in an independent, non-competitive, open-ended setting. Only basic art materials and kitchen supplies needed. (Originally published as *Scribble Cookies*.) *Scribble Art* is the primer of all Kohl's art books.

**$18.95 • 144 pages
Bright Ring • 1994 [1985]
All Ages**

MUDWORKS
Creative Clay, Dough and Modeling Experiences

MaryAnn Kohl

ISBN 9780935607024

100+ modeling and play-art ideas using play dough, mud, papier-mâché, plaster of Paris, and other mixtures from household supplies. Award Winning Best Seller. An arts and crafts classic! Voted Best of the Best.

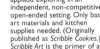

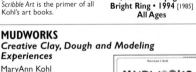

**$18.95 • 152 pages
Bright Ring • 1989
All Ages**

Process, Not Product Art Series

FIRST ART
Art Experienes for Toddlers & Twos

MaryAnn Kohl

ISBN 9780876592229

75+ art experiences are specifically designed for the little guys, including tips for success. Filled with art exploration especially for toddlers and two year olds. *1st book in the Process, Not Product art series.*

**$14.95 • 160 pages
Gryphon House • 2002
Ages 1-5**

PRESCHOOL ART
It's the Process, Not the Product

MaryAnn Kohl

ISBN 9780876591680

Over 250 process-oriented art projects designed for children 3-6, but enjoyed by kids of all ages. Uses materials found commonly at home or school. Organized by months, seasons, and art techniques. *2nd book in the Process, Not Product art series.*

**$24.95 • 260 pages
Gryphon House 1994
Ages 3-6+**

PRIMARY ART
It's the Process, Not the Product

MaryAnn Kohl

ISBN 9780876592830

100+ amazing creative art projects have results to delight and teach elementary aged children. Each activity has three parts: basic, experienced, and challenging. Promote the process of art exploration, and appreciate the individualized result. *3rd book in the Process, Not Product art series.*

**$19.95 • 190 pages
Gryphon House • 2005
Ages 5-10**

MUDWORKS – Bilingüe / Bilingual
Experiencias creativas con arcilla, masa, y modelado
Creative Clay, Dough, and Modeling Experiences

MaryAnn Kohl

ISBN 9780935607178

50+ activitiests from the original *Mudworks*, translated into Spanish and English on facing pages.

**$14.95 • 160 pages
Bright Ring • 2002**
Bilingual Edition • Edición bilingüe
All Ages

The BIG MESSY ART Book
***But Easy to Clean Up**

MaryAnn Kohl

ISBN 9780876592069

100+ adventurous activities beyond the ordinary for exploration of art on a grander more expressive scale. Hundreds of bonus variations included.

$14.95 • 144 pages • Gryphon House • 2000 • 4-12

COOKING ART

Kohl & Potter

ISBN 9780876591840

150+ artistic, edible recipes

**$19.95 • 160 pages
Gryphon House • 1997
Ages 3-10**

MATH ARTS
Exploring Math through Art for 3-6 Year Olds

Kohl & Gainer

ISBN 9780876591772

200+ art activities to introduce young children to early math concepts

$24.95 • 260 pages • Gryphon House • 1996 • 3-6+

MAKING MAKE-BELIEVE
Fun Props, Costumes, & Creative Play Ideas

MaryAnn Kohl

ISBN 9780876591987

125+ ideas for pretend and make-believe through creative art expereinces.

**$16.95 • 190 pages
Gryphon House • 1999
Ages 1-8**

GLOBAL ART
Activities, Projects, and Inventions from Around the World

Kohl & Potter

ISBN 9780876591901

135+ easy-to-do art projects that introduce kids to cultures and people worldwide.

**$16.95 • 190 pages
Gryphon House • 1998
All Ages**

PRESCHOOL ART Mini-SERIES

5 books of art fun for preschool kids & older, each book a chapter from the award winning single volume, *Preschool Art*.
64 pages each • 2001 • $9.95

- CLAY & DOUGH   ISBN 9780876592502
- CRAFT & CONSTRUCTION   ISBN 9780876592519
- PAINTING   ISBN 9780876592243
- DRAWING   ISBN 9780876592236
- COLLAGE & PAPER   ISBN 9780876592526

Bright Ring Publishing, Inc.

P.O. Box 31338 • Bellingham, WA 98228-3338
360-592-9201
WWW.BRIGHTRING.COM • INFO@BRIGHTRING.COM

BRIGHT IDEAS FOR LEARNINGtm

Order Online www.brightring.com

Bill to:

Name_____

Address_____

City_____ State_____ Zip_____

Phone (___) _____ Email_____

Ship to: *(if different from billing address):*

Name_____

Address_____

City_____ State_____ Zip_____

Phone (___) _____ Email_____

NEW

Qty.	Title of Book	Book Cost Each	Price
	ACTION ART *Hands-On Active Art Adventures*	$21.95	
	GREAT AMERICAN ARTISTS FOR KIDS *Hands-On Art Experiences in the Styles of Great American Masters*	$18.95	
	DISCOVERING GREAT ARTISTS *Hands-On Art for Children in the Styles of the Great Masters*	$18.95	
	STORYBOOK ART *Hands-On Art for Children in the Styles of 100 Great Picture Book Illustrators*	$18.95	
	MUDWORKS *Creative Clay, Dough, and Modeling Experiences*	$18.95	
	MUDWORKS EDICIÓN BILINGÜE ~ BILINGUAL EDITION *(Spanish & English in one book) Experiencias creativas con arcilla, masa, y modelado*	$14.95	
	SCRIBBLE ART *Independent Creative Art Experiences for Children (originally published as Scribble Cookies)*	$18.95	
	SCIENCEARTS *Discovering Science Through Art Experiences*	$18.95	
	GOOD EARTH ART *Environmental Art for Kids*	$18.95	
	COOKING ART *Easy Edible Art for Young Children*	$19.95	
	FIRST ART *Art Experiences for Toddlers and Twos (1st in 3-book series)*	$14.95	
	PRESCHOOL ART *It's the Process Not the Product (2nd in 3-book series)*	$24.95	
	PRIMARY ART *Art Experiences for Kids 5-10 (3rd in 3-book series)*	$19.95	
	THE BIG MESSY ART BOOK **But Easy to Clean-Up*	$14.95	
	MAKING MAKE-BELIEVE *Fun Props, Costumes, and Creative Play Ideas for Kids to Make and Do*	$16.95	
	GLOBAL ART *Easy Edible Art for Young Children*	$16.95	
	MATHARTS *Exploring Math through Art for 3-6 Year Olds*	$24.95	
	PAINTING: *Preschool Art 5 book Mini-Series*	$ 9.95	
	DRAWING: *Preschool Art 5 book Mini-Series*	$ 9.95	
	CLAY & DOUGH: *Preschool Art 5 book Mini-Series*	$ 9.95	
	CRAFT & CONSTRUCTION: *Preschool Art 5 book Mini-Series*	$ 9.95	
	COLLAGE & PAPER: *Preschool Art Mini-Series*	$ 9.95	
	SNACKTIVITIES *50 Edible Activities for Parents and Young Children (from the original, Cooking Art)*	$ 9.95	
	GREAT COMPOSERS FOR KIDS *Composition, Instruments, and Musical Art Activities (AVAILABLE 2016)*	N/A	

SHIPPING CHART

USPS Media Rate (10 days) (US Postal):	UPS Ground -or-1st Class Priority (US Postal):
$5.00 first book in box + $3.00 each additional in same box	$8.00 first book in box + $3.00 each additional in same box

CALL FOR CUSTOMIZED SHIPPING NEEDS OR INTERNATIONAL RATES

Please make checks payable to **Bright Ring Publishing, Inc.**
Prefer credit card? Call 800-788-3123 • orderentry@perseusbooks.com

Book Amount	
Shipping Amount *(See Chart)*	
Subtotal *(Book Amount plus Shipping Amount)*	
Washington State Residents Only **Sales Tax** 8.9% *on Subtotal*	
TOTAL ENCLOSED *(add WA Tax plus Subtotal)*	

Please pay by check to Bright Ring Publishing, Inc.

To remove order form, tear here